Getting Started with Enterprise Internet of Things: Design Approaches and Software Architecture Models

L. S. Jayashree • G. Selvakumar

Getting Started with Enterprise Internet of Things: Design Approaches and Software Architecture Models

Springer

L. S. Jayashree
Department of Computer Science
and Engineering
PSG College of Technology
Coimbatore, Tamil Nadu, India

G. Selvakumar
Computer Science and Engineering
Sri Shakthi Institute of Engineering
and Technology
Coimbatore, Tamil Nadu, India

ISBN 978-3-030-30944-2   ISBN 978-3-030-30945-9 (eBook)
https://doi.org/10.1007/978-3-030-30945-9

This Springer imprint is published by the registered company Springer Nature Switzerland AG.
The registered company address is: Gewerbestrasse 11, 6330 Cham, Switzerland

Preface

The Internet of Things (IoT) paradigm is making the world smarter by connecting every possible device or 'thing' to the Internet. It enables communication and data exchange across the household appliances, industrial machinery, medical equipment and several other electronic devices. This technology has opened doors to revolutionary breakthroughs. Smart cities, smart industries, smart education, smart healthcare and smart services are some of the terms that became popular recently due to the advancements of the Internet of Things in several areas. The quality of life and the quality of work are expected to be immensely benefited by incorporating the Internet of Things in our daily life and in the enterprises. The Internet of Things applications are classified into two broad categories which are Domestic IoT and Enterprise or Industrial IoT. Though technically they are similar, they are completely different in terms of their magnitude, the number of users, the scope of revenue generation, the size of applications, its impact in society, etc.

This book approaches the Internet of Things with an enterprise perspective. The first two chapters provide a detailed introduction to the Internet of Things technology. The networking protocols involved in the IoT and the cloud solutions for the Internet of Things are discussed in detail. And we have a separate chapter to discuss the edge computing which is significantly changing the way the end-to-end IoT applications are designed. Chapter 4 introduces the use of the Internet of Things in enterprises with the help of few sample applications, and it analyses the differences between Enterprise IoT and Domestic IoT. The various components of an Enterprise IoT solution, challenges and winning strategies in developing them are discussed in this chapter. The architectural concerns of Enterprise IoT are discussed in Chap. 5. The middleware layer concerns and the two different popular options for architecting the solutions – Monolithic and Microservices architectures – are touched upon in the same chapter. Various aspects related to the design and implementation of Enterprise IoT are handled in Chap. 6 with discussions related to the recent advancements like Big Data, Artificial Intelligence and Block Chain. The next and final chapter is dedicated to discuss about the various development platforms in the market today which are being used to implement the End-to-End Enterprise IoT solutions. Throughout the book, we have included case studies to understand the Enterprise IoT in a more practical viewpoint.

Coimbatore, Tamil Nadu, India L. S. Jayashree
Coimbatore, Tamil Nadu, India G. Selvakumar

Acknowledgments

L. S. Jayashree
I want to profusely thank my institution, PSG College of Technology, for the support and motivation to author this book. I would like to express my love and gratitude to my beloved mother, supportive husband, and my inquisitive children, Athish Thirumal and Shasticka Thirumal, for silently offering their moral support in all my professional endeavors. I want to heartily acknowledge the contributions of my colleague Dr. S. Suriya in Chap. 2, and the support of my research scholars Ms. Iswarya and Ms. Madhana in drawing the diagrams.

I would like to bring out this book in loving memory of my father late Shri. L. Subramanian, an intense reader and a passionate writer. In spite of his expression of interest several times to proofread my manuscripts, I unfortunately failed to get benefited from his knowledge and services at the end. Had he been alive today, he would have proofread this book to absolute perfection!

G. Selvakumar
I would like to acknowledge with gratitude the support and guidance provided by my research supervisors and my institution who kept me motivated in the process of writing this book. Also, I thank my family and friends for their continuous encouragement throughout the work.

Contents

Chapter 1
The Internet of Things: Connectivity Standards

Abstract In the present Internet of Things (IoT) era, we are continuously witnessing an increasing number of the objects around us becoming smart and having the capability of sensing, processing and exchanging the data collected from its ambience. The IoT protocols can be broadly divided into two major groups: (i) IoT connectivity protocols and (ii) IoT messaging protocols. When it comes to connectivity standards, there is a plethora of options available for IoT application developers. Wireless connectivity standards that are already existing like Bluetooth, WiFI, LTE etc. along with those that are designed especially for IoT like LoRa, 6LowPAN are discussed in this chapter. Though not exhaustive, this chapter gives an extensive coverage of the most popular IoT networking protocols.

Keywords IoT communication standards · Bluetooth low energy · Zigbee · 6LowPAN · WiFi · LoRa

Learning Objectives

1. To understand the basic architecture of IoT and get a big picture about the need for various communication standards
2. To get a detailed insight about the different wireless connectivity options available for IoT developers, their pros and cons
3. To understand the applicability of different communication standards in typical use cases

1.1 Introduction

Internet of Things (IoT) refers to a platform through which uniquely identifiable embedded computing devices or things can be connected to the Internet or to each other. By means of connecting these devices through a common platform, they can be monitored continuously, their performance can be analysed, can be controlled

L. S. Jayashree, G. Selvakumar, *Getting Started with Enterprise Internet of Things: Design Approaches and Software Architecture Models*,
https://doi.org/10.1007/978-3-030-30945-9_1

from a remote place and they can collaborate with each other in a federated manner so as to deliver better experience and value added services to its end users. The end users can be individual consumers, a system, a public service, an industry or a business. Internet of Things is an amalgamation of advancements happening in connectivity hardware, data networks, cloud computing, artificial intelligence, big-data processing etc. The number of connected devices already exceeded 20 billion and by 2020, the number is expected to reach 50 billion with an estimated 19 trillion dollars of IoT business.

It is no longer a fantasy today to listen to stories like your T-shirts talking to the washing machines helping it to decide the optimum amount of water and detergent to be used for perfectly cleaning the dirt in your shirt or your grandma who is living alone in the native being prompted to take her prescribed medicines when she misses a dose and also get tele advice for her queries related to a minor health complication she developed last night. Internet of Things based wearable assistive devices are a revelation of the rapid advancements happening in the field of embedded systems and greatly help in improving the Quality of Life (QoL) of the elderly population and people with special needs. Connected health care is just one use case of IoT but there are other physical systems like buildings, oil wells, wind mills, factories, transportation systems, power grids and so on which are increasingly becoming smart by means of computing and communication elements that are embedded into it. These physical things are thus connected to the cyber world so that their working status can be monitored, their performance can be analyzed and they can collaborate with other physical systems creating a greater intelligent outcome and bring more value to the users of those things. Businesses and enterprises can gain a competitive edge and earn better profits by means of being able to derive actionable and intelligent insights about the status and behaviour of the various working elements involved.

A simple snapshot of the making of a cyber-physical system is shown in Fig. 1.1 as a series of layers, where raw data from a physical thing moves up in the digital value chain and contributes to build a digital service. The raw data, as it moves up in the hierarchy gets transformed as useful knowledge and key insights about the working status / condition of the physical system under consideration.

A typical big picture of Internet of Things (IoT) architecture shown in the Fig. 1.1, consists of real world objects and things equipped with sensors and actuators to monitor a given real world phenomenon. The raw data collected from the physical things and objects over a period of time are intelligently processed using data analytics techniques so as to derive some useful insights about the phenomenon under observation.

The transformation enabled by IoT in connecting the physical world of machines and the virtual world of Information Technology (IT) and in integrating all areas of the industry is what is cited as the 'Industrial Internet of Things'. The Industrial Internet enables organisations to use the various connected components of loT such as sensors, Application Programming Interfaces (APIs), software platforms, data analytics to gather and analyse data, are helpful to optimize business operations and provide value-added services to its customers.

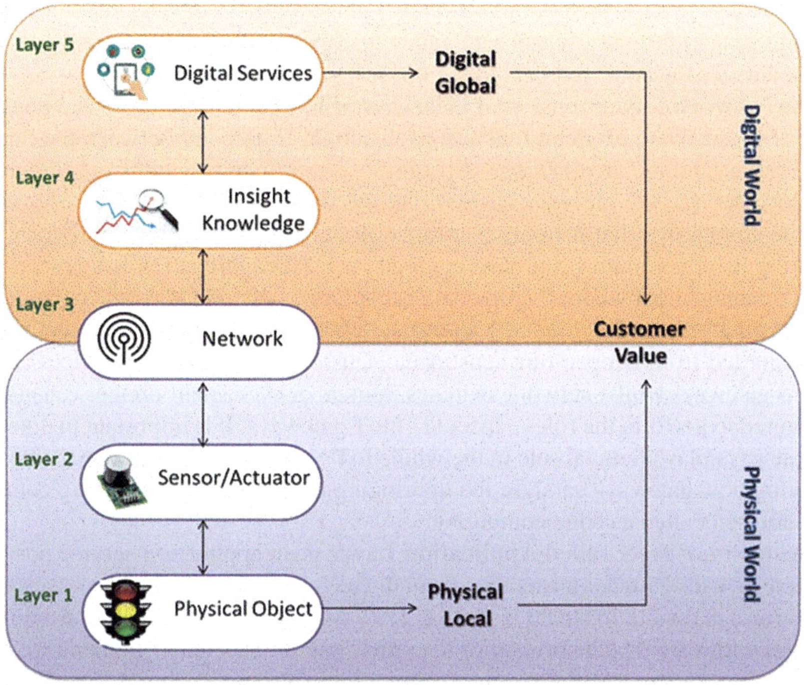

Fig. 1.1 A big picture of IoT digital value chain

The IoT control loop starts with connecting things, monitoring the various parameters / operating conditions of the device, analysing the gathered data to gain useful and actionable insights about the overall performance of the system under study and ends up in controlling the operating conditions autonomously to achieve desirable conditions. The above four elements of the IoT control loop ultimately leads to better value to the various stakeholders of the system. For end users, it gives better value for money, improved experience, increased service life, autonomy of operation etc. For the producers of the device or for the remote administrators, it gives real time insights about the device's location, status of operation, likelihood of failures, usage patterns of the device etc. It enables the enterprises to build better business models around the usage patterns of the device and thereby earning better profits and gain a competitive edge over its rivals.

1.2 The IoT Architecture

The IoT architecture can broadly be studied in terms of three layers, namely, the **Things layer**, **Network layer** and **Application layer**.

The Things layer is the bottom most layer that comprises of sensors such as temperature sensor, pressure sensor etc. and actuators, which gathers sensed data and communicates the collected data to the upper layer.

The **Network Layer** consists of Gateways or IoT hubs. A gateway is a physical device or a software program that acts as the connection point between the remote cloud server and the smart things. All sensed data moving to and from the cloud, traverses through the gateway. Sensed data from the Things layer will eventually become so massive that it imposes a threat in delivering it to the cloud, therefore requiring local computing and data aggregation. Data aggregation is a crucial part of data management where the raw data is captured, accumulated and summarized before being sent to the cloud. e.g. computing hourly average of temperature readings recorded from temperature sensors etc. Custom built hardware devices can be used as gateways whilst network switches, routers or even smart phones can also be configured to perform the roles expected of IoT gateways. It is important to note that the gateways play a crucial role in the whole IoT ecosystem and in Chap. 3, we will be seeing how gateways catalyse the upbringing of the new and emerging computing paradigm called as edge computing.

The top most layer called **Application Layer** is an application service provider that is responsible for acquiring data from the sensors and, if essential, converting it to a format that suits IoT data analytics. Data Analytics is a process of examining data sets with varying data properties to extricate significant and actionable business insights that are normally represented in the form of trends, patterns, and statistics to execute effective decision-making processes. This is the layer which contains the various use cases built to leverage the power of IoT to give better services to the individual consumers or improved public services to a society, or better profits to businesses.

1.3 The IoT Communication Models

Referring to the architecture given in Fig. 1.2, the sensors in the sensing layer send their observed data to the gateway for further processing. Normally gateways are positioned closer to the operating environment or one hop away from the devices e.g. an IoT hub in a smart home environment or a network switch in a smart factory setting. Hence, either wired/wireless Local Area Networking standards (LAN) or Wireless Personal Area Standards Networking (W-PAN) are used for connectivity between sensors/actuators and the gateway devices.

In most of the IoT use cases, the data aggregated by the gateways are sent to a remote cloud server for performing historical analysis, data visualization and reporting. This normally requires the involvement of either LAN communication standards or long distance communication effected through 3G/4G mobile Internet standards or other Wide Area Networking (WAN) standards.

As mentioned in Fig. 1.2, the wireless radio communication standards used to bridge between Sensing layer and Network layer are LAN and PAN standards and

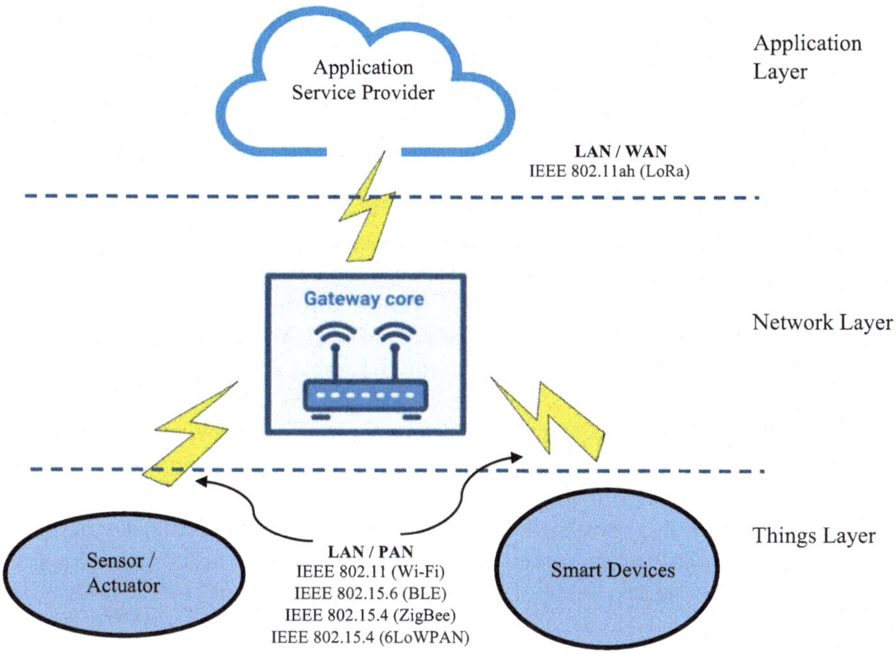

Fig. 1.2 IoT communication model

the platform between Network layer and Application Layer are LAN and WAN standards.

- LAN Standards
  - Wi-Fi
  - Ethernet
- PAN Standards
  - Bluetooth Low Energy (BLE)
  - ZigBee
  - 6LoWPAN
- WAN Standards
  - LoRa
  - LTE, VoLTE and the upcoming 5G

Wi-Fi is a wireless signalling or communication used for the Wireless Local Area Networking (WLAN) devices based on the IEEE 802.11 family of standards. **BLE** is a wireless personal area network technology on the IEEE 802.15.4 standard aimed at improving the battery life time of the smart objects and reducing the cost. The **ZigBee** standard extends 802.15.4 to provide Bluetooth-like interoperability features suited for high-level communication protocols used to create personal area networks with small, low-power digital radios having higher lifetime than Bluetooth and Z-Wave.

6LoWPAN standards enable the efficient use of IPv6 over low-power wireless networks on simple embedded devices on carrying IPv6 or IPv4 data packets over the IEEE 802.15.4 standards thus providing seamless connectivity to a huge variety of networks.

A wide area network (WAN) is a telecommunications network that extends over a large geographical separation for networking. **LoRa** is a long-range wide area network protocol that achieves extremely long range connectivity designed especially for Internet of Things. Besides, the well-established mobile data standards like 2G (GSM/ GPRS/CDMA), 3G(UMTS, EDGE, W-CDMA, LTE) and 4G (VoLTE) already have the infrastructure to run IoT applications over it. An example of this rapid evolution in the GSM architecture during the last 10 years is the introduction of WWAN technologies every 18 months beginning with GPRS in 2001, EDGE in 2003, UMTS in 2005, HSPDA in 2007, HSUPA in 2008, and HSPA 7.2 in 2009, and now LTE and VoLTE.

The evolution of this ecosystem has enabled utilities to support legacy network implementations while at the same time introduce newer and faster network capabilities as needed. The upcoming 5G standard is expected to make a break-through in the IoT space as IoT is envisioned as one of the major use cases of 5G. Taking into account the ever increasing bandwidth requirements owing to the massive data produced by the millions of IoT devices, 5G is considered as one of the key technology enablers of IoT.

The subsequent sections discuss some of the popular IoT networking protocols. The mobile Internet WAN standards spanning across second generation to fifth generation are beyond the scope of this chapter. Interested readers are requested to refer appropriate resources that discuss these standards in detail.

1.3.1 Communication Standards to Build IoT

1.3.1.1 Bluetooth Evolution

The original Bluetooth standard, named as Classic Bluetooth in the literature, is popularly known for its ability to connect peripheral devices to a computer system and for sharing streaming video and audio across Bluetooth enabled devices. Understandably, the problem with the classic Bluetooth is its high power consumption and hence its inability to withstand for longer periods of operation.

Bluetooth Low Energy, abbreviated as BLE, is mainly aimed at reducing the power consumption of the Bluetooth enabled devices whilst maintaining the same coverage range of classical Bluetooth. BLE also uses the same unlicensed 2.4 GHz

ISM band like most of the other WPAN standards. BLE was formerly branded and marketed as *Bluetooth Smart* and apparently aimed at the Internet of Things (IoT) market, where very low chunks of payload need to be transmitted. BLE is targeted at applications that require low energy consumption enabling the devices to run unattended for longer periods of time- even for several months together.

Bluetooth Smart was adopted in 2010 and this evolved as a separate standard. Hence, it did not turn out to be backward compatible with Classic Bluetooth. This leads to a situation where a Bluetooth headset not being able to connect to a smart watch, which is BLE enabled. This includes the former modes, Basic Rate (BR) and Extended Data Rate (EDR), and also carries Bluetooth Low Energy along with the standards of the former protocols up to Bluetooth version 3.0 in order to provide backward compatibility and interoperability with the former standards. BLE supports a data rate of 3 Mbps. [1] BLE serves a plethora of novel applications like home automation, smart door locks, connected lighting systems, healthcare, wearable devices, security systems and home entertainment use cases.

A device can support multiple BLE profiles like Bluetooth healthcare profiles, sports and fitness profiles, Internet Protocol support profiles and environmental sensing profiles. Bluetooth 4.2, released in 2014 aimed at pairing with emerging IoT devices, includes features like low energy, secured communication, link layer privacy with improved scanner filter policies including the latest version profile called Internet Protocol Support Profile (IPSP).

Bluetooth 5, released in 2016, mainly focuses on providing better support for IoT use cases especially in home automation and smart factory applications. It has doubled the transmission speed of up to 2 Mbps and extended advertising message size and advertising range to reach a significant distance of about 240 m. Communication between the Bluetooth devices and its role in Internet of Things are further explained in this chapter with an illustration using BLE in a Voice based Remote control IoT application.

1.3.1.2 BLE Devices Types

BLE devices are basically of two types:

- **A Central Device** – device with more compute, storage and power capabilities
- **Peripheral Devices** – devices with constrained power supply, compute and storage capabilities

Devices like smart phones, tablets, laptops etc. can act as the Central device while sensor nodes, smart things and other low energy wearable devices are examples of BLE Peripheral devices. Central device has a very high duty cycle compared to peripheral devices while the peripheral devices are made to sleep most of the time. This is the main key behind saving power in BLE (Fig. 1.3).

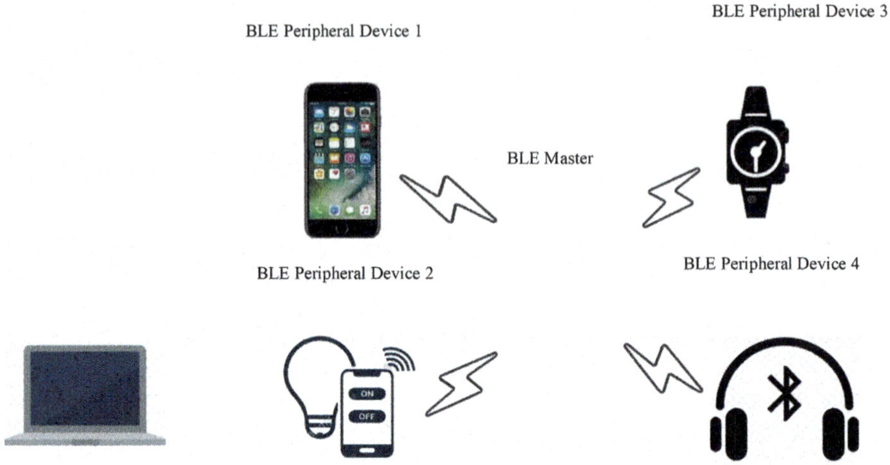

Fig. 1.3 A BLE connection event

1.3.1.3 BLE Connection Modes

BLE devices can converse with devices available in their vicinity in one of two different ways: (i) **Broadcasting mode** and (ii) **Connection mode**. Two BLE devices can exchange data in a periodic manner using a BLE Connection which is point-to-point and bidirectional. The central device initiates a BLE connection when it finds an advertising packet sent by a peripheral device 1 as shown in Fig. 1.3.

Upon initiating a connection, similar to the hopping sequence used in classical Bluetooth standard, the central device decides the timing sequence to be followed by the peripheral devices for synchronized data exchange with the central device that acts as the master. The peripheral devices should follow the timing sequence determined by the master in order to exchange data with the master. Because of following a predetermined timing sequence, the peripheral devices just need to be awake during their scheduled data transfer timings (called as connection event) and go to sleep during the rest of the periods and comes back up during the next connection event. The protocol sequence is illustrated in Fig. 1.4.

1.3.1.4 BLE Packet Types

BLE devices can send two different kinds of packets:

- **Advertising Packets**
- **Scan Response Packets**

Advertising Packets are important and are continually being transmitted from a peripheral device so as to be seen by different devices. In BLE standard, there are

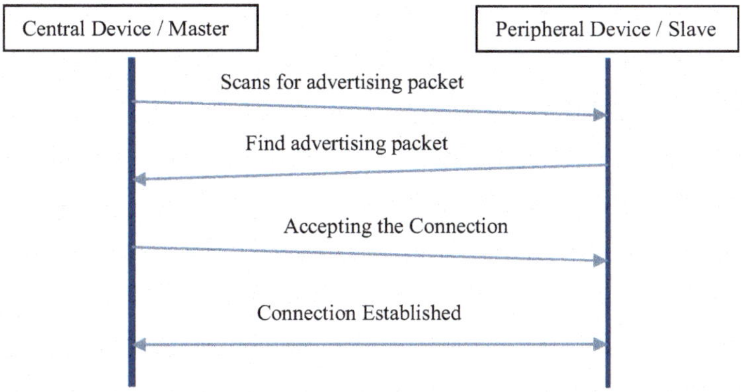

Fig. 1.4 BLE timing sequence

totally 40 channels, each 2 MHz wide; out of these 40 channels, 3 channels are primarily dedicated for sending advertisements (channels 37, 38 and 39). Channels 0–36 are used for data transfer after initiating a connection event. At the point when different devices get advertisement packets, they can demand extra information from the peripheral device which at that point sends the Scan Response Data.

Similar to known conventions, a BLE device uses Broadcasting to send data to multiple devices at the same time. In the BLE Broadcasting mode, a device performing the role of *Broadcaster* sends advertisement packets to all the listening devices called as *Observers* as per BLE literature. When an observer finds an advertisement packet during its repeated scanning process, it initiates the Scan Response Mode to further know more about the data being broadcast.

Having discussed about the pairing between

(i) Central device with peripheral devices and
(ii) Broadcaster with Observers,

it is essential to understand at this point that a single device can simultaneously perform multiple roles. For example, a smart phone can act as a broadcaster for sending announcements to multiple smart wearable devices in a wellness management IoT application; at the same time, it can additionally act as a peripheral device to the nearby gateway or an IoT hub which does the role of the central device.

The Major Features of BLE

The following are some of the main benefits of BLE:

- Low energy consumption
- Low cost
- BLE chips are available in almost all smart phones

BLE is not suitable for high data rate applications involving streaming audio and video. Rather, it is suitable for data emerging from small sensor based devices. The range is typically limited to 50–150 m line of sight. BLE 5 extends the range up to

800 m line of sight. Theoretically, the speed of the BLE is the same as that of classical Bluetooth, which is 1 Mbps. However, Bluetooth version 5 doubles the data rate, and hence we get up to 2 Mbps. Having said this, it is important to note that, when the application demands long range communication, then the speed of data transmission has to be traded off. Longer the range, lower is the data transmission speed. It may be reduced to the range of 500–125 kbps, for instance, depending on the communication range of interest. But all the above mentioned figures are only theoretical data rates, practically, what the application gets for the actual payload transmission is even lower, because of the packet overheads introduced by the intermediate layers.

1.3.1.5 Bluetooth Mesh

Bluetooth Mesh is the newest addition to the Bluetooth family, which got released in 2017. Mesh was introduced to extend the range of Bluetooth connectivity and support many to many connections, which is quiet typically required in many industrial IoT applications. In a Bluetooth mesh topology, a BLE device can initiate connections with multiple devices simultaneously. Having said this, they don't really establish multiple point to point connections, but rather they use the advertise and scan mode to relay messages to multiple devices in its vicinity.

Nodes

A device that is part of a Bluetooth mesh is called a Node and a device that is not part of the mesh is called an *unprovisioned Device*. An unprovisioned device, once gets provision to join the mesh becomes a node. A node now can have multiple elements which can be controlled independently. For example, in a smart home environment, in a connected light scenario, different lights can belong to different elements and thus can be set with different properties and be turned on during different times of the day, with different brightness levels, for different durations and so on. This bring in a better control over the environment and here is where Bluetooth tries to mimic the capabilities of zigbee.

The Publish- Subscribe Model in Bluetooth Mesh

In order to exercise more flexible control over the different smart devices, say, in a smart home environment, Bluetooth mesh uses a Publish-Subscribe model similar to MQTT protocol which is already a well established messaging protocol in IoT based applications. Assuming that there are ten smart switches and a set of smart appliances to be controlled using these switches, as illustrated in Fig. 1.5, form a Bluetooth mesh. Now utilizing the Publish- Subscribe method, a node may send messages to multiple appliances using the Publish protocol. Subscription is the act of receiving messages from a selected switch(es).

For example, the smart speaker can receive signals both from switch 1 and switch 2. Similarly, both switch 5 and switch 6 and both control the connected lights fixed in the garden area.

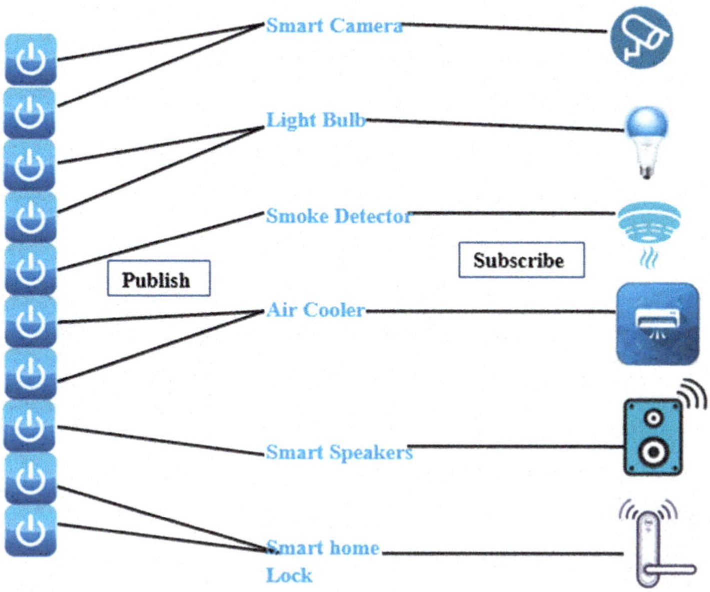

Fig. 1.5 The publish- subscribe model in bluetooth mesh

1.3.1.6 A Sample Case Study: BLE Applied Voice Based Remote Control

Remote controls have turned out to be significantly more than basic point and press devices. As television set top boxes and other individual hardware include greater usefulness, remote controls include more User Interface abilities that are becoming increasingly user friendly. A sample application that utilizes Texas Instrument's CC26xx devices makes it simpler to configure by offering a one chip answer for Bluetooth Low Energy network, voice enabled control, and MCU integration is shown in Fig. 1.6.

1.3.2 Zigbee

Having discussed about Bluetooth Low Energy, it is now time to look at a more powerful and versatile WPAN standard, which is commercially known as Zigbee. Zigbee was initially developed as a wireless sensor network standard and later turned itself as one of the major enablers of IoT. It has been making rapid strides in the home automation, building automation as well as industrial automation space. Zigbee is based on IEEE 802.15.4 standard which describes Low-Rate Wireless Personal Area Networks (LR-WPANs). IEEE 802.15.4 standard was defined specially for devices that feature short range, low cost, low data rate, low processing power, limited memory and low power. It is used to create personal area networks

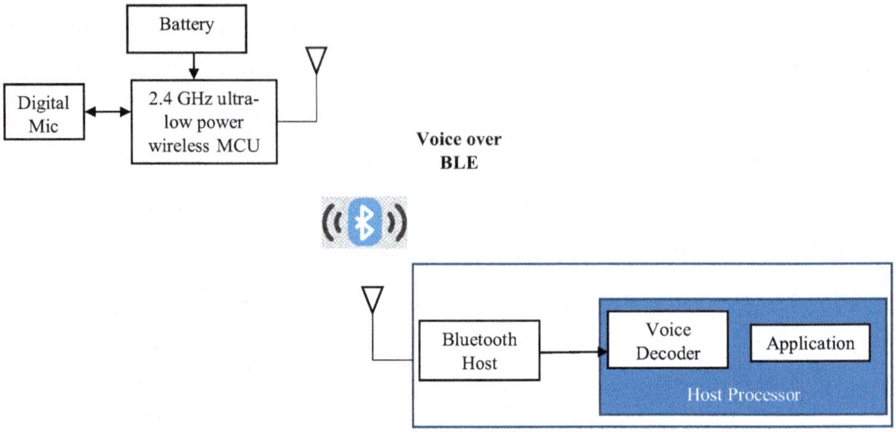

Fig. 1.6 Voice based remote control using BLE in IoT environment

with small, low-power digital radios, such as those meant for home automation, assisted living environments, smart energy and other low-power and low-bandwidth needs, designed for small scale automation projects. Zigbee predominantly uses the license free 2.4 GHz band but nevertheless in some parts of the world it also uses 866 MHz and 915 MHz also. In 866/916 MHz band, it provides 20–40 Kbps and in 2.4 GHz it provides 250 Kbps.

ZigBee transmits the data at the rate of 250 Kbps (2.4 GHz), 40 Kbps (915 MHz) and 20 Kbps (868 MHz) of the original data throughput to meet the demands of low bit rate data transmission. The advantages of ZigBee are low price, small size, and it uses relatively small bandwidth. The disadvantages of the ZigBee are the small battery that limits its lifetime, small memory, limited data rate and low processing capability. Moreover, its operation in the unlicensed frequency of 868 MHz and 2.4 GHz may have interference with other Wi-Fi, Bluetooth and Microwave signals.

While there are many wireless communication standards available for meeting the demands of high bandwidth application, like the LAN standards such as WiFi, wide area mobile Internet options such as LTE/VoLTE standards as shown in Fig. 1.7, the designers of zigbee found that there was a considerable gap in the low data rate, short distance coverage options. Of course, BLE standard that was discussed in the previous section covers this gap but nevertheless, since it operates at average speed of up to 1 Mbps, despite bearing the tag as Bluetooth Low energy, it still expends higher power and hence the device life time is restricted. Besides, Bluetooth supports only eight active devices and up to a maximum of 256 parked mode devices in a single network while Zigbee supports as many as 65,536 devices in a single network. As Zigbee connection needs to offer a speed of up to 250 kbps, its low power utilization confines the transmission distances to 10–100 m line-of-sight. Because of this restricted coverage, the device life time is extended to several months which is very high when compared to BLE.

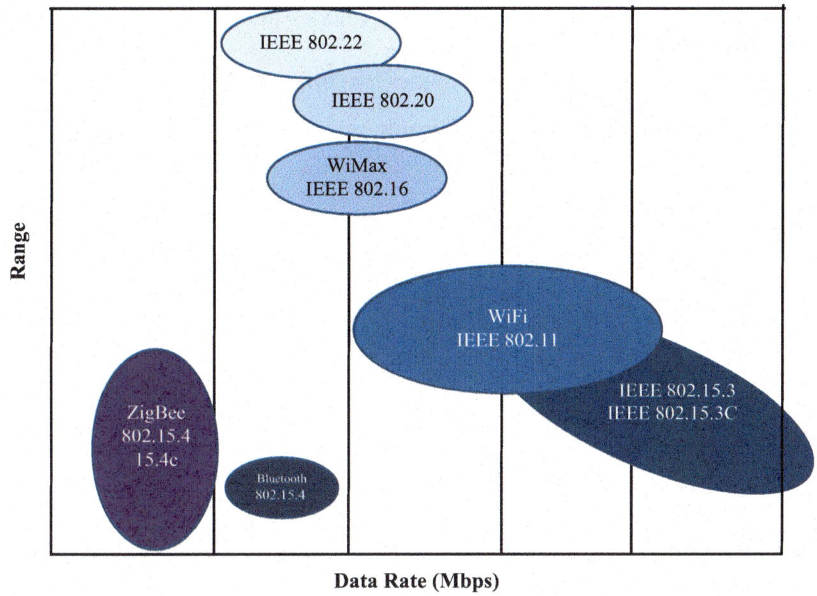

Fig. 1.7 The Juxtaposition of Zigbee in wireless communication standards space

1.3.2.1 The Zigbee Protocol Stack

The Zigbee alliance, a non profit consortium [2], whose members are wireless network product companies, OEMs, communication standards people etc., have made noteworthy efforts with the following objectives:

- Make the standard commercially successful
- The products developed based on the standard can interoperate with each other and
- The technology can sustain for longer periods of time.

Such consortia and their efforts help to make sure that the companies who develop products based on the given IEEE or IETF standard earn better business values for their products. In short, as shown in the Fig. 1.7, while the original IEEE 802.15.4 standard defined the Physical and Medium Access layers, the Zigbee alliance subsequently brought out the Network layer, Security layer and a set of Application Programming Interfaces (APIs) which together acts as the middleware between the applications and the underlying zigbee network. The middleware part defined by the Zigbee Alliance is the key behind realizing customized application profiles for multiple IoT use cases supported by Zigbee standard.

Zigbee networks provides security at the network layer level and encrypts the entire network frame using AES-128 encryption standard. The Application Interface Layer (API) acts as the interface between the applications and the underlying network. The ZDO layer is responsible for local and over the air management of the network. It provides services to discover other nodes in the network and is responsible for the current state of the network.

At the application layer, Zigbee provides two different types of profiles:

(i) Manufacturer specific application profile
(ii) Public application profile

Manufacturer specific application profile:

- Allows a device vendor to develop customized products using a ZigBee Compliant Platform
- Certification testing makes sure that the developed product can interoperate with other ZigBee devices
- Vendor specific applications cannot interoperate at the application layer

Public application profile

- Allows products developed by different vendors for a given public profile can interoperate with each other
- Gives flexibility to product vendors to add value added features to the existing public profiles

A Zigbee device can support upto 240 application objects which are called as Zigbee Device End points.

1.3.2.2 ZigBee Device Types

The zigbee architecture consists of the following three types of devices:

- ZigBee Coordinator
- ZigBee Router
- ZigBee End Devices

A given ZigBee device can act either as a Full Functional Device (FFD) or as a Reduced Function Device (RFD). A device acting as FFD implements all the tasks defined by the 802.15.4 standard. An RFD implements only partial functions. Obviously, devices that have the luxury of unconstrained power supply can act as a FFD.

The **ZigBee Coordinator (ZC)** is the most powerful device. There is one ZigBee Coordinator in each system and it is a Full Functional Device.

The coordinator performs the following functions:

- Selects the channel to be used by the network
- Starts the network
- Allocates addresses to nodes or routers
- Permits other devices to join or leave the network
- Holds a list of neighbors and routers
- Transfers application packets

The **ZigBee Router (ZR)** is also a Full Function Device (FFD) used to expand network coverage. The function of a router is to find the best route to the destination over which to transfer a message. A router performs all functions similar to ZC except establishing the network.

ZigBee End Device (ZED) is a Reduced Function Device (RFD) that operates within a limited set of the IEEE 802.15.4 MAC layer, enabling it to consume less power. The end device (child) communicates only through a router or a coordinator. It also operates at low duty cycle power, meaning it consumes power only while transmitting data. Therefore, ZigBee architecture is designed so that an end device transmission time is short.

The end device performs the following functions:

- Joins or leaves a network
- Transfers application packets

1.3.2.3 The Zigbee Topologies

In star topology, the Zigbee coordinator is the central device to which all the other devices, including the Zigbee routers are connected. All the communication happens only through the central coordinator which is the main drawback of this topology despite its simplicity.

In a Zigbee tree, the Coordinator automatically becomes the root and can have Routers as their children. A Router can have End nodes as their children as depicted in Fig. 1.8. Such a strict hierarchical arrangement effects the children to communicate only with their parents. The shortcoming in such an arrangement is that, if a parent is down, the children become(s) disconnected from the rest of the network.

In Zigbee mesh, there is one coordinator, several routers at the same level which communicate with each other in a peer-to-peer fashion using a multi hop communication. Understandably, this is the most resilient topology when compared to tree and star, as there are multiple alternate paths available for communication. A mesh arrangement extends the network coverage while shorter communication distances

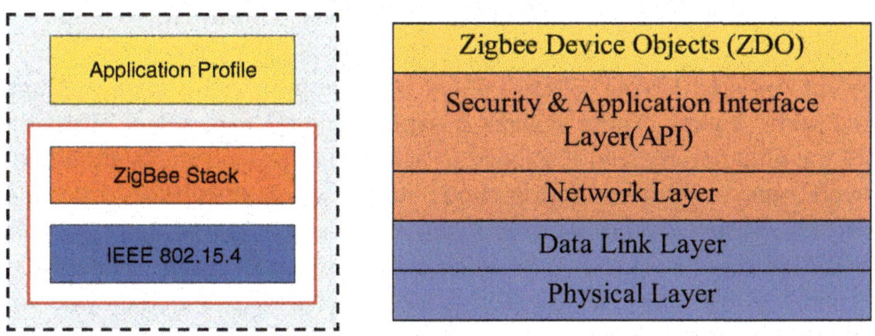

Fig. 1.8 The zigbee protocol stack

between nodes improves the network life time, which make this topology a popular choice for Zigbee nodes. Zigbee devices can cover long distances by passing data through a mesh network of intermediate devices to reach more distant ones.

1.3.2.4 Data Transfer Modes in ZigBee

Data Transfer between the PAN Coordinator and End device is made possible using the following two modes:

- Beacon Enabled
- Non Beacon Enabled

In **Beacon Enabled Networking**, contention free channel access strategy is utilized. Here, the Coordinator distributes a specific time slot vacancy to every device, known as Guaranteed Time Slot (GTS). Here, each of the devices in the system should be synchronized. This is guaranteed by sending a Beacon signal from the coordinator to every device (hub), with the end goal that every device synchronizes its clock. However, this may end up diminishing the battery life of devices when in no other assignment than synchronizing their clock.

When the device is synchronized, it can transmit information to the coordinator utilizing Carrier Sense Multiple Access with Collision Avoidance (CSMA-CA). On sending a request, the Coordinator sends back the acknowledgement. For exchange of information from Coordinator to device, an indication is sent with the Beacon message to the device. The device at that point gets this indication and sends a data request message. The Coordinator sends an acknowledgement of this data request receipt and exchanges the corresponding data.

In **Non-Beacon Networking**, the Coordinator does not transmit any Beacon message. Rather, every device transmits data utilizing CSMA-CA technique in a similar frequency channel. The device transmits the information when the channel is clear. For exchange of information from Coordinator to device, the end device initially sends a data request message to the Coordinator and then transmits the data message with a null length payload, on accessibility of data.

1.3.2.5 A Sample Case Study: ZigBee Healthcare Monitoring System

In Ambient Assisted Living, elderly people can be monitored using implanted or wearable body sensors. These sensors monitor the vital parameters of the patient. Some of the vital parameters of interest to health care professionals are blood pressure, heart rate, oxygen saturation, body temperature, respiratory rate and gait parameters acquired through wearable inertial sensors. These signals are collected through the appropriate sensors embedded in the different wearable medical devices as shown in Fig. 1.9. These are the Zigbee End Devices (ZED) and they acquire the bio signals from the different types of medical devices and the gathered signals are

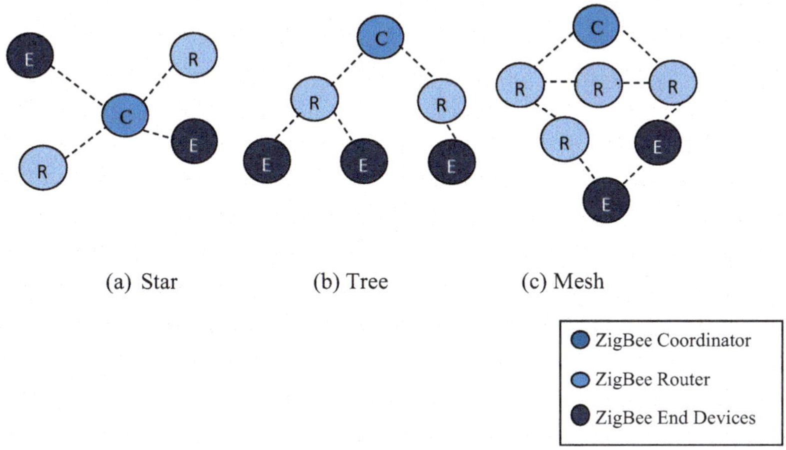

Fig. 1.9 Different zigbee Topologies

then sent to the Zigbee Coordinator (ZC) through Zigbee Routers (ZR) which are positioned in specific places to act as relays.

ZC transmits the aggregated biosignals to the cloud server for further processing and distribution to remote health care centers. Use cases like telemedical care, tele medical advice, remote patient monitoring, long term elderly care etc. can be built around the gathered medical data for effective patient care.

The following are some of the advantages from such assisted living solution for elderly in independent living settings:

- Patients can remain in their own home and long hospital waiting for routing check ups is avoided
- Doctors can adjust medication levels online and more accurately assess the effectiveness of a therapy
- Allows continuous wellness monitoring of elderly family members
- Sense movement or activity monitoring of elderly
- Notify via mobile phone when anomalies occur
- Wireless panic buttons for falls or during other emergency situations

Zigbee 3.0

In order to provide users with more value added services and developers with more flexibility in building applications, Zigbee 3.0 has come up with the following feature that makes it better preferred over the earlier versions:

- Provides interoperability among devices belonging to multiple application profiles:
  - For example, a humidity sensor from Zigbee HVAC profile can co-exist with an occupancy sensor of Zigbee Security profile

- Includes testing, certification, branding and marketing support to make it easier to develop and sell interoperable products and solutions
- It is built on Zigbee PRO, which is an enhancement of 802.15.4 standard by adding mesh networking and security features along with the application framework thus providing single stack solution.
- Supports connectivity with legacy LAN and WAN networks, thus improving interoperability further among multiple systems.

1.3.3 6LowPAN

6LoWPAN is the acronym for IPv6 over Low-Power Wireless Personal Area Networks. This is the standard that makes IP packets to be carried over the standard WPAN networks defined by the IEEE standard 802.15.4. Having IP, more specifically IPv6, as the core communication protocol makes this standard unique and distinct from the rest of the wireless networking technologies designed for wireless ad hoc sensor networks and IoT. The wedlock between IPv6 and the 802.15.4 is primarily focused on empowering low data rate and low duty cycle embedded devices to leverage the existing Internet infrastructure. The RFC 4919 release of Internet Engineering Task Force (IETF) 6LoWPAN working group has made the use of IPv6 over the IEEE 802.15.4 possible. By virtue of this unique aspect, 6LoWPAN is considered as one of the key competitor of ZigBee.

1.3.3.1 6LoWPAN for IoT

While 6LoWPAN can be used in general for many IoT based automation applications, it is specifically designed to empower long distance IoT communication that leverages the existing Internet infrastructure. One of the best example use cases is the way the smart meters from individual homes can be connected to a smart grid operator's infrastructure using an IP backbone network. [5] Of course, Smart grid operations and connected street lights are envisioned as some of the promising applications of 6LoWPAN.

Those familiar with traditional networking standards are sure to be quiet familiar with the success model behind of Internet Protocol (IP). IP is known for its simplicity, flexibility and versatility and can literally carry any type of payload, be it text or voice or video. IP can run on top of any underlying networking technology as well. Hence, allowing the smart IoT devices to participate in the Internet and carrying the payload generated by such sensor based devices shouldn't be a problem for IP. But nevertheless, as IP v4 is running out of address space, accommodating the tiny sensor nodes and allocating them individual IP addresses is completely ruled out. But given the fact that IP v6 uses a mammoth 128-bit address space and is not exhaustible in the foreseeable future, it does have the luxury of giving away unique IP v6 addresses to our smoke alarms, washing machines, smart meters and even to our tiny smart watches. This allows each of these smart devices to be queried and controlled directly from a remote monitoring entity.

Another advantage of IP is its mesh networking capability which makes it robust against link and node failures by making use of alternate paths for routing data, hence it is said to be *self-configuring* and *self-healing*.

The 802.15.4 based wireless PANs are characterized by the following features:

- Most commonly uses 2.4 GHz and also uses 915 MHz and 818 MHz in some parts of the world
- Packet size is 127 bytes, leaving only 81 bytes for payload leaving the layer overheads
- Connections are unreliable
- Devices sleep most of the times to save energy

1.3.3.2 The 6LoWPAN Architecture

As shown in Fig. 1.10, the 6LoWPAN architecture adopts the bottom two layers from the IEEE 802.15.4 standard. The IPv6 protocol is used as the network layer protocol in 6LoWPAN.

1.3.3.3 The Adaptation Layer

In order to make the IPv6 network layer compatible with the MAC layer of IEEE 802.15.4, an adaptation layer is introduced between the network and MAC layers. It performs fragmentation and reassembling of IPv6 packets, IPv6 header compression, and addressing to enable compatibility. The adaptation layer is the key ingredient in the success of 6LoWPAN.

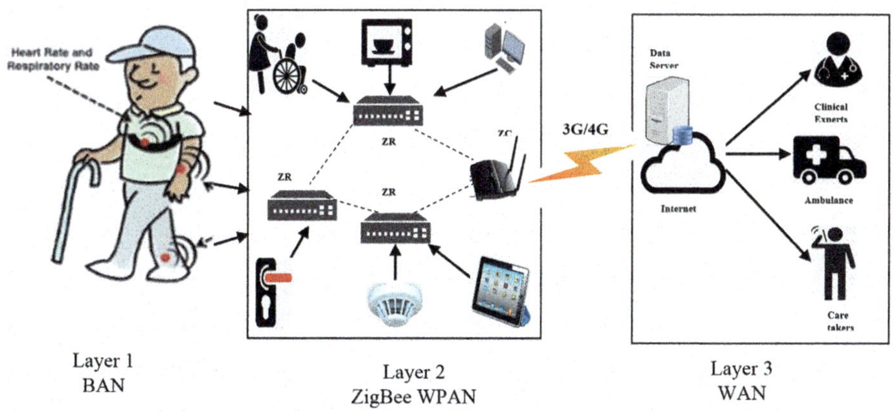

Fig. 1.10 Wearable health monitoring using zigbee

In order to adapt to the low power wireless network environments which carry only very short data units so as to save power, that is to send IPv6 packets over 6LowPAN, the IP packets which can be theoretically up to 1280 bytes, should be fragmented into smaller units in order to be carried over wireless PAN data units. This is being handled by the adaptation layer.

The next major function of this layer is the TCP/IP header compression. This is required again due to fact that the WPAN networks can handle only a maximum size of 128 bytes. Given the fact that the IP header alone constitutes 40 bytes, UDP header adds another 4 bytes and the fragmentation process adds another 5 bytes overhead, an application payload cannot be carried over by the WPAN network without header compression.

1.3.3.4 The Role of Edge Routers

The 6LoWPAN network shown in Fig. 1.11 consists of edge nodes which obtain IP address assignment form the Edge Router. In case of moving sensor nodes, the concept of mobile IP is used wherein it gets dynamic IP addresses assignments from the edge router which is currently responsible for serving the mobile sensor node. The nodes can move within the same 6LowPAN network, or from the vicinity of edge router to another or between different 6LowPAN networks (Fig. 1.12) [5].

The conceptual design of a home automation network using 6LoWPAN is shown in Fig. 1.5. The main objective is to develop a home automation network that is robust, compatible with other connectivity standards and easy to configure with value added features. Such system allows the smart home users to monitor and control wireless connected devices such as smoke sensor, light etc., through Wi-Fi. A gateway core is implemented to help interoperability between heterogeneous 6LoWPAN and legacy IP networks based on Ethernet or Wi-Fi and also provides consistent interface. Remote users traverse internet facility till Gateway core is reached. Later, using 6LoWPAN wireless communication to the home devices is facilitated.

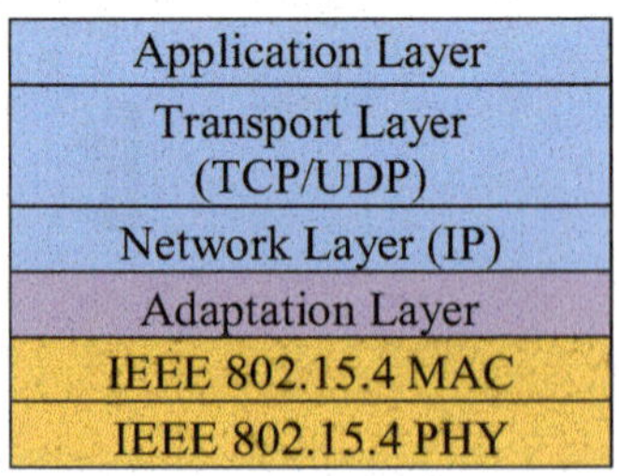

Fig. 1.11 6LowPAN network architecture

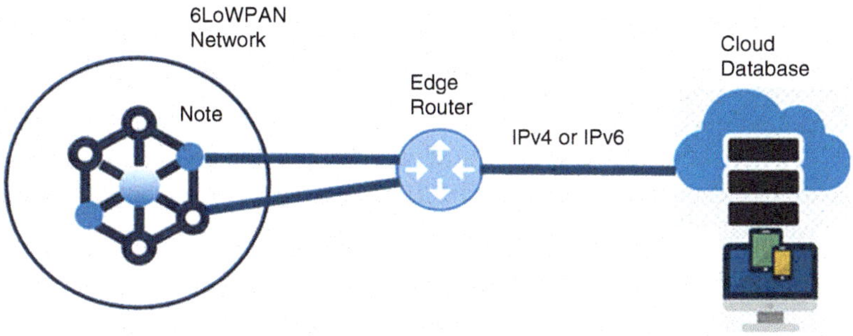

Fig. 1.12 6LOWPAN network connected through edge router

Table 1.1 Comparison between Zigbee and 6LoWPAN

Feature	Zigbee	6LoWPAN
The PHYand MAC layers	Based on IEEE 802.15.4	Based on IEEE 802.15.4
Number of addressable nodes	Served by 32 bit address space	Served by 128 bit address space
Compatibility with internet protocol	No	Yes
	Devices cannot directly communicate with internet	Compatible with IPv6. Devices can directly participate in internet
Topologies	Star, mesh, tree and cluster star	Tree and mesh
Frequency spectrum	2.4 GHz (250 kbps), 915 MHz (40 kbps) and 868 MHz (20 kbps)	2.4 GHz (250 kbps), 915 MHz (40 kbps) and 868 MHz (20 kbps)
Header compression	No header compression or fragmentation mechanism applied	Reduction of protocol overhead by header compression and fragmentation
Security protocol	AES-128	AES-128

1.3.3.5 ZIGBEE vs. 6LoWPAN

The following table summarizes the similarities and differences between the two most popular IoT communication standards, namely ZigBee and 6LowPAN (Table 1.1) [6].

1.3.4 Wi-Fi

Wi-Fi is a group of radio technologies used for Wireless Local Area Networking (WLAN) devices based on IEEE 802.11 standards. IEEE 802.11 wireless LANs use a media access control protocol called Carrier Sense Multiple Access with Collision Avoidance (CSMA/CA). Wi-Fi is a trademark of the Wi-Fi Alliance and Wi-Fi based devices including desktops, laptops, smart phones, smart TVs, modern printers, digital audio players etc., can connect to the Internet through a WLAN and wireless gateway called hotspot that covers about a range of 20 m. This coverage distance can be improved by utilizing multiple overlapping access points. Wi-Fi commonly operates at 2.4 GHz UHF and 5.8 GHz SFH ISM radio bands to transmit data across a network, achieving speeds of over 1 Gbps. A personal computer should have a wireless adapter to convert digital data into a radio signal and this radio signal is transmitted through an antenna to a decoder called the router, eventually to the Internet through a wired Ethernet.

1.3.4.1 Wi-Fi in IoT

Internet of Things application has distinct connectivity requirements in terms of range, data throughput, energy efficiency and device cost. Wi-Fi is always an evident choice in building IoT since the coverage is almost ubiquitous. Data transfer requirements for IoT vary from small, intermittent payloads from utility meters to large amounts of continuous data such as real-time video surveillance. Range requirements can span from very short distances for wearable devices to several kilometers for applications like weather forecasting, agriculture monitoring, off shore oil and gas pipeline monitoring etc. Wi-Fi or IEEE 802.11, is a wireless LAN standard built with the intent of replacing Ethernet using wireless communication over unlicensed bands. Its main objective is to provide off-the-shelf, easy to implement, easy to use short-range wireless connectivity with cross-vendor interoperability. Each Wi-Fi access point can handle up to 255 connected devices. [7] An IoT environment may contain huge number of devices barring the fact that the access point has a maximum supportable limit. By deploying multiple access points, more number of devices can be connected. These huge number of devices in the IoT environment leads to interference and generally, Wi-Fi provides a high degree of interference immunity. Over five billion Wi-Fi-enabled devices are used worldwide and Wi-Fi Alliance manages the certification requirements to insure certain standards of interoperability required in Internet environment.

1.3.4.2 A Sample Case Study: WiFi in Civil Structures Health Monitoring System

The ability to monitor a structure and detect damage at the earliest possible stage has been of great interest to the engineering communities because it permits the safety of valuable human lives and the conservation of economic resources. The need for structural health monitoring of civil constructions arises from deterioration/aging of structures, adaptation of existing structures to new design standards, mistakes in design/construction, overloading, and changes in functionality requirements of structures. The structural monitoring system provides real-time information to help quickly identify damages and the severity of damage which can lead to quick decision on immediate repairs, interruptions or continuous use of the structure. This is a vital tool that will help to reduce the incidence of building collapse in developing nations.

A real time, on-site sensing technology to analyse the service characteristics of RC buildings for the purpose of early detection of structural damages and impending failures can be built using IoT. It involves the observation of the given RC structure over time using periodically measured data from an array of sensors in the following manner:

1. Periodic inspection of cracks using conventional instrumentation
2. If structural defects e.g. internal cracks in structural members, corrosion in rebars etc. are suspected, deploy smart aggregate sensors (SAS) to continuously monitor the rate of growth of structural cracks, corrosion, ingress moisture level, carbonation depth etc.
3. Transmit the data wireless to a local coordinator node wireless using zigbee communication standard (IEEE 802.15.4)
4. Aggregate the data locally at the coordinator node to minimize communication overhead
5. Generate alerts when the monitored parameters exceed preset threshold levels
6. Send aggregated reports to cloud based Remote Server at scheduled intervals using WiFi (IEEE 802.11b) or GSM
7. Employ advanced machine learning algorithms at the remote server to predict the rate of growth of crack and corrosion
8. Generate necessary visualization through charts, reports etc. about the strength of structural members of interest

The overall block diagram of the various elements involved in the complete structural integrity monitoring system comprising of (i) the wireless sensors (ii) a local on-site gateway for preparing summaries about the data and (iii) a cloud based remote server for long term data archiving, predictive modeling and reporting of insights to the concerned stakeholders.

As shown in Fig. 1.13, the data acquisition module receives signals from various different sensors attached to different critical and strategic locations of the structure under study. The sampling module converts the received voltage signals into digital voltages, and transmits them to the cluster head through WiFi (IEEE 802.11b) protocol through the RF module. The cluster head node performs local data processing and aggregation (e.g. taking average of sampled parameters), generates alerts when necessary. Advanced signal processing algorithms are employed subsequently to understand the nature, location and severity of probable defects in the structure and the higher level message digest is sent to the Remote Monitoring System using mobile Internet/WiFi standard.

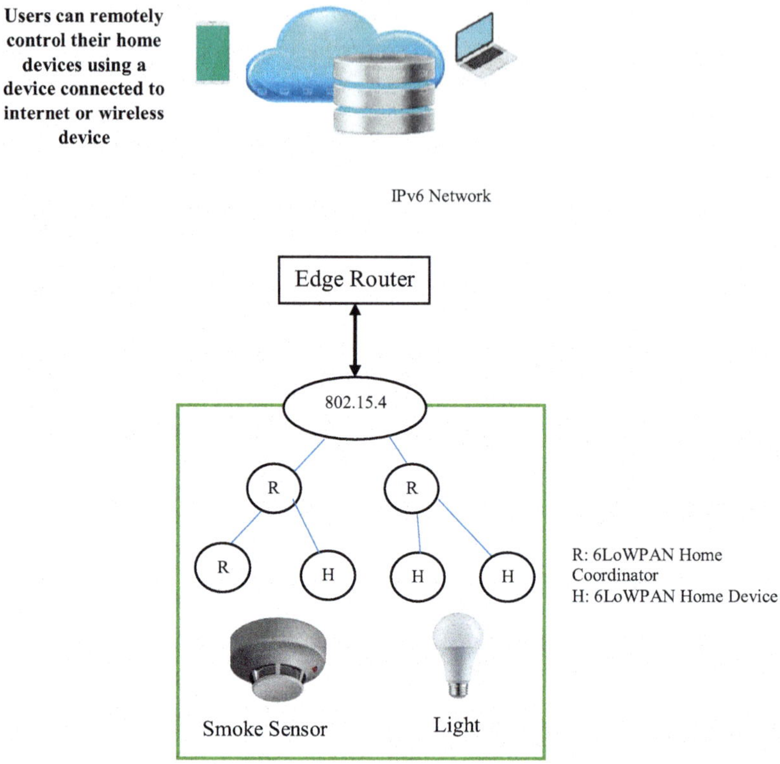

Fig. 1.13 6LoWPANHome automation network

1.3.5 LoRa

LoRa (Long Range) is a patented digital wireless data communication technology. LoRa is a long-range wireless communication protocol that is also known as Low Power Wide Area Network (LP-WAN). LP-WAN enables the huge number of IoT devices to connect to the Internet; the WAN part of LP-WAN implies that it is determined to achieve very long range connectivity unlike the previously discussed PAN and LAN standards like BLE, Zigbee, 6LowPAN and WiFi.

LoRa achieves extremely long range connectivity, to an extent of several kilometres, greater than that achieved by wide area mobile Internet standards like GSM, UMTS, LTE and VoLTE. Such a very high range of coverage is achieved by means of trading off the network bandwidth, or in other words, the data rate. There is an inverse relationship that exists between bandwidth and achievable communication range. Hence, if we want to achieve increased communication range, we need to reduce the data rate. LoRa allows a maximum data rate of 27 kbps which is far less than the other wireless communication standards we discussed in this chapter. Apparently, LoRa is suitable for applications involving wireless sensor nodes generating only few bytes of data, like temperature monitoring, soil moisture monitoring etc. LoRa is clearly not suitable for applications involving high bandwidth real time surveillance data or for self-driving cars, considering the nature of data and amount of data generated by such applications every given second.

LoRa chips transmit in the sub-gigahertz spectrum (109 MHz, 433 MHz, 866 MHz, 915 MHz), which is an unlicensed band that has less interference than others like the 2.4 GHz range used by Wi-Fi, Bluetooth and other protocols. At those frequencies, signals penetrate obstacles and travel long distances while drawing relatively little power and hence, ideal for many IoT devices, which are often constrained by battery life.

Within the sub-GHz spectrum, LoRa chips use a spread-spectrum strategy to transmit at a variety of frequencies and data rates. That allows the gateway to adapt to changing conditions and optimize the way it exchanges data with each device. The following table shows the frequency spectrum used by LoRa in different parts of the world.

Frequency	Region
868 MHz	Europe
915 MHz	North America
433 MHz	Asia

It should be noted that it does not use the universally adopted license free ISM band which is centered around 2.4 GHz and hence a LoRa device should be bought in a region specific manner. Besides, even though the above mentioned frequencies are license free bands in the corresponding regions, it does come with a price. A LoRa can use only 25 mw of power which is extremely low and offers a data rate in the range of 50 bps to 50 kbps.

1.3.5.1 The LoRaWAN Architecture

The LoRaWAN architecture is depicted in the Fig. 1.14. The architecture shows how a huge number of end devices are connected to a each LoRa gateway. The devices in the LoRaWAN network can transmit low bandwidth messages up to a distance about 5–15 kms for several months to a few years (Fig. 1.15) [3].

The LoRaWAN gateway shown in the architecture connect to the end devices, which are enabled with LoRa radio shields, using a LoRaWAN network and on the other end, the gateways connect to the back bone infrastructure using high bandwidth networks like LTE, WiFi etc. around which multiple LoRa applications like smart water, smart transportation, smart energy are built. The single most unique aspect of LoRaWAN is that, a single gateway is sufficient to cater to the communication needs of thousands of end devices which are available a few kilometers away. The gateways are equipped with concentrators to receive packets from huge number of end devices.

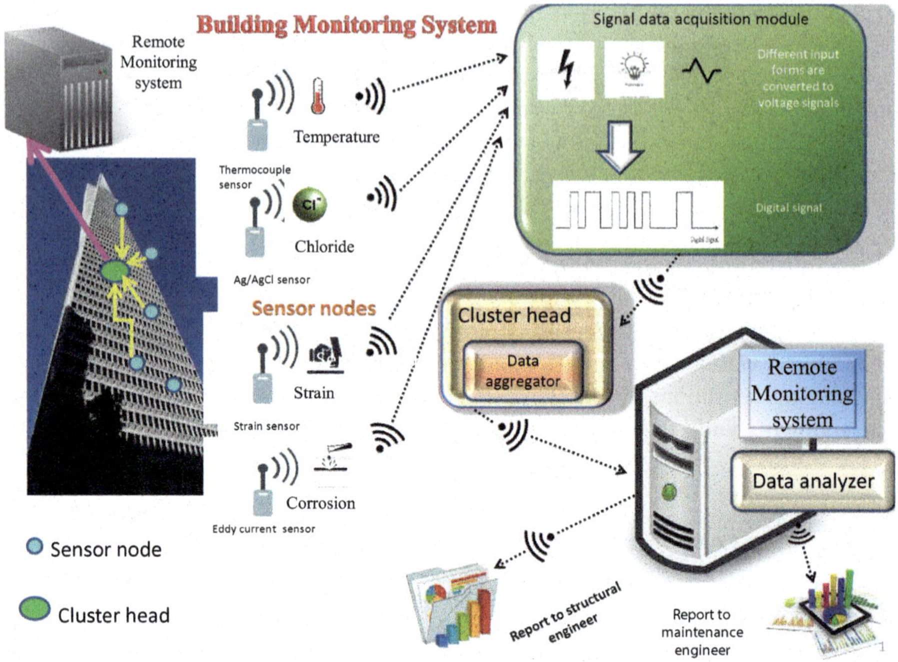

Fig. 1.14 Overall block diagram of the wiFi based civil structures health monitoring system

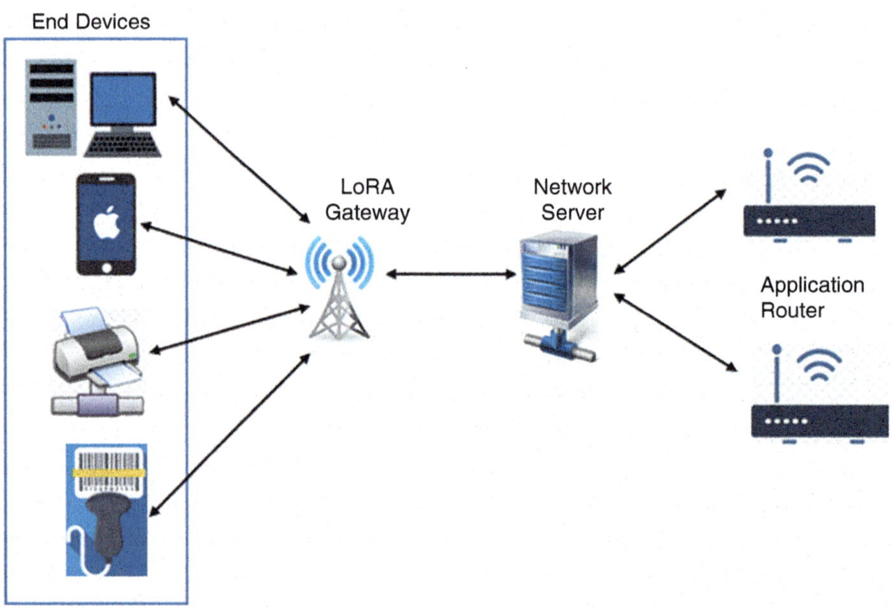

Fig. 1.15 The LoRAWAN architecture

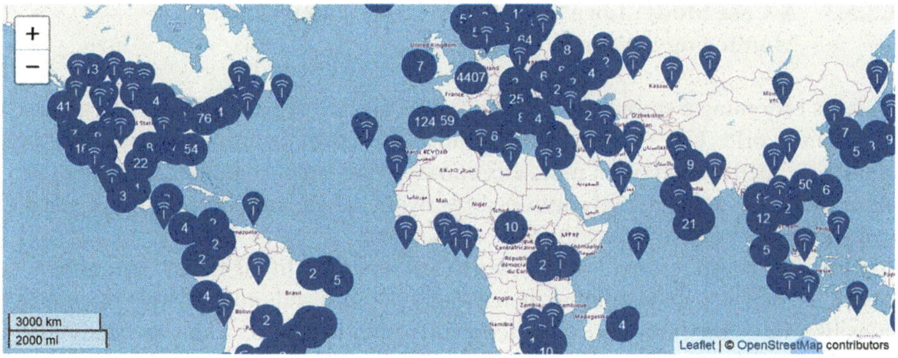

Fig. 1.16 Current snapshot of LoRA gateways geospatial mapping. (Courtesy: [4])

A LoRa gateway can be installed either on commercial basis or community basis. The community approach relies on interconnecting the distributed gateways that are privately built and maintained. The Things Network [4], abbreviated as TTN, leads a community approach to build a worldwide, open, crowd sourced LoRaWAN network. TTN provides a live map of available LoRa gateways across several regions of the world as shown in Fig. 1.16. This is helpful for anybody who want to operate a LoRa device to check whether their region is served by a LoRa gateway. It also encourages private operators to install their LoRa gateways in a region which currently has no coverage, so that this gateway can be used by multiple other applications subsequently. A recent press release from Netherland says that it has the world's first nationwide LoRa network built for IoT.

1.3.5.2 LoRa: An Ideal Choice for Smart City Projects

Smart city represents a nervous system of connected objects that collect data with which the assets and resources are efficiently managed to enhance the quality of living. It provides digital services to support many public activities and utilities. For the sustainable communication, the physical objects require low power network which is the backbone of smart city. LoRa, a long range low power wireless technology is a perfect choice for such intermittent low data rate connectivity over long distances (10–15 kms) with better battery performance (~10 years). It is deployed in numerous smart city applications such as smart metering and lighting solutions, structural health monitoring system, smart water leakage detection, smart flood sensors, parking management, smart lighting, energy and pollution meters, fire detection systems, traffic signal management, self-driving cars, etc.,

In the US, several cities like Philadelphia, San Francisco, Chicago and Charlotte are implementing IoT for its various urban services. Taiwan has chosen LoRa protocol for smart city deployment. Many cities in India are also using LoRa technology for developing smart city projects. Using IoT, the world is getting more connected and LoRa paves a better way to perform it.

1.3.5.3 A Case Study: LoraWAN Based Lake Water Quality Monitoring System

Water is becoming a shrinking commodity and in short supply in many cities across the entire world. Use of hazardous chemicals in manufacturing industries, dying industries, textile and cotton mills etc. cause severe water pollution, as waste from these industries goes directly into nearby rivers, lakes and ponds without getting treated to remove harmful toxins and compounds.

Laboratory testing of water samples to assess its quality is time consuming and laborious. Sensors are becoming increasingly popular and more reliable in applications like air quality monitoring, water quality monitoring etc. This case study illustrates a low cost sensor based monitoring device for continuous real time water quality monitoring of all the water bodies available in and around a given city. It is proposed to make use of low cost sensors for monitoring the basic water quality related parameters, namely, Temperature, pH, dissolved Oxygen, Turbidity and Electrical Conductivity integrated with open source development boards like Arduino/Raspberry PI, to result in a low cost, autonomous real time water quality monitoring device embedded into Lotus shaped robotic devices to float around the water body and make spatially distributed observations periodically. Each bot is embedded with LoRa radio shield to connect to the LoRa gateway and transfer the time- tagged and geo- tagged sensor readings as shown in Fig 1.17.

The floating lotus bots deployed in each lake carry sensors with proper shielding and packaging for measuring the basic water quality parameters such as pH, temperature, dissolved oxygen, turbidity and electric conductivity. Water quality

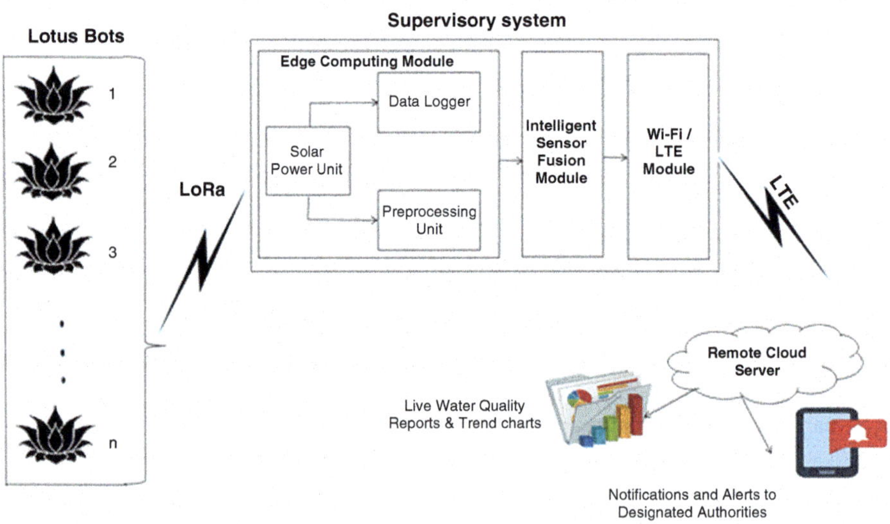

Fig. 1.17 Lotus bots: the low cost water quality monitoring device

indicative parameters from the different sensors attached to the lotus bots can be gathered at the supervisory stations using LoRa. The supervisory station then computes the daily summaries of the various quality parameters and sends it to the remote cloud server for detailed analysis and reporting using LTE standard. The real time water quality data of all the water bodies in the city can thus be continuously tracked through web application and mobile application.

The Supervisory Module

The centralized Supervisory Module configures and controls the on-site lotus bots, as necessary. It performs the following actions:

- ***Data logger module*** – collects and stores the periodic measurements of the different water quality parameters
- ***Edge Computing Module*** – based on an *ensemble of machine learning algorithms* for intelligent aggregation of multi modal sensor data, it prepares high level message digest about the water quality measurements
- ***Communication module*** - the high level information derived out of the edge computing module will be transmitted to the remote cloud server through LoRA wireless standard.

Web Based Data Management with GIS Mapping and Advanced Analytics

It generates diagnostic reports, trend charts etc. with GIS mapping, to give fine-grained spatio-temporal water quality data and water quality scores of the different water bodies under study to the interested stakeholders. This data can be tracked continuously online through a web application and a mobile application.

This module also takes care of intelligent post processing of aggregated sensor data using a combination of statistical, machine learning and fuzzy inference techniques to predict the *likely course of the water quality deterioration* and *generate alerts* as and when necessary.

1.4 Conclusion

This chapter presented a detailed discussion about the most popular wireless connectivity standards available in the present scenario for the IoT system developers pertaining to the devices to gateway communication and from gateway to the remote cloud server communication. The choice of a particular communication standard depends on the range of communication, bandwidth requirements, cost and power consumption constraints, reliability of operation etc. Fig. 1.18 gives a summary of the available connectivity standards in a nutshell.

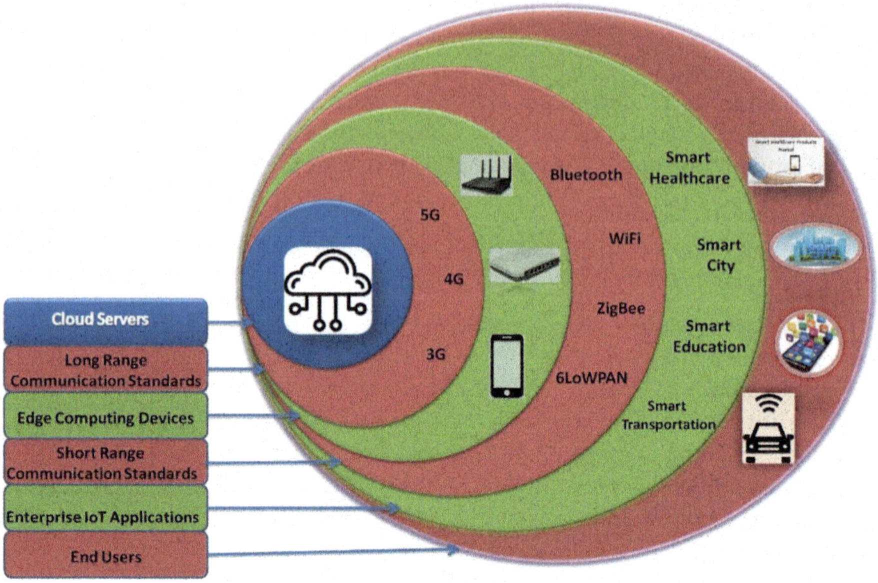

Fig. 1.18 Wireless communication technologies in a nutshell

References

1. https://en.wikipedia.org/wiki/Bluetooth_Low_Energy
2. https://www.zigbee.org
3. https://lora-alliance.org
4. https://www.thethingsnetwork.org
5. https://en.wikipedia.org/wiki/6LoWPAN
6. https://www.plugintoiot.com/what-is-6lowpan/
7. https://www.wi-fi.org

Chapter 2
Cloud Solutions for IoT

Abstract Internet of Things (IoT) paradigm paves the way of connecting every object with the Internet environment to share information that improves the quality of life. On the other hand, the cloud computing facilitates pay per use model by providing on demand delivery of computing resources. The IoT can gain unlimited resources and computing capabilities from the cloud and the cloud can step ahead in its way towards the real life scenarios in a dynamic and distributed manner. This chapter introduces the role of cloud computing in IoT and discusses the need to integrate IoT and cloud, highlighting its benefits and implementation challenges. It also emphasizes the role of evolution of cloud based IoT systems towards federated ecosystems and its architecture, requirements and challenges

Keywords Cloud computing · IoT cloud · Virtualization in IoT · Monolithic IoT cloud · Vertical supply chain · Federation

Learning Objectives

- To interpret why IoT and cloud are inseparable
- To understand the contributions and challenges in IoT cloud integration
- To understand the problems existing in cloud based IoT platforms
- To gain sufficient knowledge about the IoT supporting technologies and cloud service framework
- To learn the role of evolution of cloud based IoT systems towards federated ecosystems
- To get to know the architecture, requirements and challenges of IoT cloud federation

L. S. Jayashree, G. Selvakumar, *Getting Started with Enterprise Internet of Things: Design Approaches and Software Architecture Models*,
https://doi.org/10.1007/978-3-030-30945-9_2

2.1 Introduction

Cloud computing is known for its huge storage capacity, processing and security features. IoT is known for working with and addressing the challenges of real-world distributed devices with its limited processing power and storage. Many day-to-day social problems can be addressed because of the convergence of Cloud and IoT.

2.2 Cloud

National Institute of Standard and Technologies (NIST) defines clouding as: "Cloud computing is a model for enabling ubiquitous, convenient, on-demand network access to a shared pool of configurable computing resources that can be rapidly provisioned and released with minimal management effort or service provider interaction." Cloud computing model involves leasing of virtualized resources on-demand due to its availability of unlimited storage and processing capacities at a lower cost. This takes cloud computing to a higher level of providing both economic and technical benefits.

The backbone of cloud computing is its layered architecture and service driven models provided by it. The cloud architecture involves four layers as shown in Fig. 2.1. Cloud computing comprises of three service models such as Software as a Service (SaaS), Platform as a Service (PaaS) and Infrastructure as a Service (IaaS).

The Hardware Layer
It comprises of resources such as routers, servers, switches, cooling systems and power that can be physically managed and controlled. Eg: Data center.

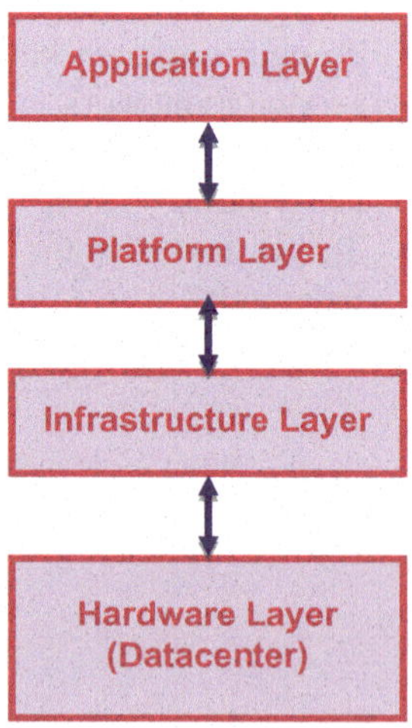

Fig. 2.1 The layered architecture of cloud computing

The Infrastructure Layer
It is responsible for managing a pool of computing and storage resources. These physical resources are partitioned to create virtual machines to service the consumer. It provides IaaS to the users on demand. IaaS is the hosted delivery of services such as hardware, network and servers to the user. Eg: Amazon EC2.

The Platform Layer
It contains operating systems and applications. PaaS deals with the delivery of complete platform and tools to develop and deploy applications to the customer. Eg: Microsoft Azure

The Application Layer
This is the layer with which the end users interact. The actual cloud provisioning is done and the user gets SaaS through it. SaaS is the hosted delivery of software which can be accessed by the user. Eg: Google Apps, Facebook

There are four types of clouds, namely, Private Cloud, Public Cloud, Community Cloud and Hybrid Cloud. Usually Private Cloud is owned, managed and operated by an individual organization by itself. Public Cloud is the one in which third party service provider makes cloud resources available to the general public and it may be free or pay per use. Community Cloud is utilized by specific community of users for their common purpose. Hybrid Cloud involves a combination of any of the above three cloud architectures.

2.2.1 Attributes of Cloud Computing and IoT

The attributes of both cloud computing and IoT need to be examined separately in order have a better understanding and clear picture of feasibility of their integration. The attributes taken for comparison of Cloud Computing and IoT are depicted in Fig. 2.2.

Storage Features of cloud computing are relatively unlimited when compared to that of IoT which has limited storage capability.

When it comes to the nature of accessibility, the data can be accessed any time with respect to cloud computing but restricted in case of IoT.

The processing speed of Cloud computing is in terms of huge power whereas limited power in IoT.

Cloud computing deals with virtual objects and IoT deals with real-world objects.

The level of accessibility of data is very flexible in Cloud computing as it can be done from anywhere at any time and limited distance with respect to IoT.

Cloud computing involves centralized components whereas IoT is concerned with heterogeneous components.

Cloud can efficiently handle and manage huge volume of data, called big data.

Cloud computing has comparatively more security features than that of IoT.

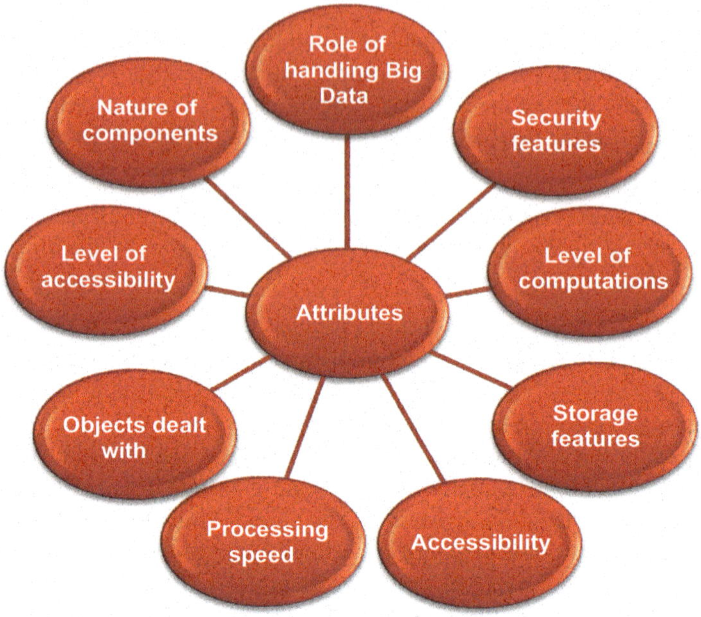

Fig. 2.2 Attributes for comparing cloud computing and IoT

2.2.2 Problems of Integration

H. Takabi et al. [1] has addressed security and privacy services of cloud computing along with the issues related to security and privacy solutions. The security and privacy landscape changes of cloud computing will impact its successful and widespread adoption. S. Subashini and V. Kavitha [2] has focused on role of safety while working cloud computing. Security is visualized as a major issue of concern for customers because it reduces the growth of cloud and evolves with complications with respect to data privacy and data protection. Awareness of adverse effects of improved features of existing security setup over important features of existing is also addressed.

J. Gubbi et al. [3] gave a wonderful perspective of evolution of IoT through sensors and actuators. Wireless Technologies has transformed IoT to fully integrated future Internet. This emerged form of IoT is implemented via Cloud platform Aneka. G. Suciu et al. [4] has described how the distributed nature of cloud computing infrastructures adds credits to IoT. The real-time application involving Smart city services are rendered by cloud provisioning effectively. This cloud services manages and controls IoT devices like sensors, actuators and other related smart devices. J. Zhou et al. [5] has focused on a common model called CloudThings, to integrate IoT (known for enabling communication via ubiquitous networks) with cloud computing (provisioning resources on demand). This model provides IaaS, PaaS, SaaS services for IoT applications. M. Soliman et al. [6] has implemented

Smart Home applications by integrating Internet of Things and Cloud computing services. The model focuses on sandwiching knowledge into sensors and actuators using Arduino platform, networking using Zigbee technology, Cloud services enabling interactions with smart things, improving data exchange efficiency using JSON data format.

M. Aazam et al. [7–9] focuses on the need of integrating IoT and Cloud computing called as "Cloud of Things". In addition to that, the authors also highlighted the issues that may arise due to this integration. Those issues include protocol support, energy efficiency, resource allocation, identity management, IPv6 deployment, service discovery, quality of service provisioning, location of data storage, security and privacy and unnecessary communication of data. A smart gateway communication model is implemented as a fusion of IoT and cloud computing to have an efficient utilization of power. This smart gateway device helps in better utilization of network and cloud resources. It is used to transmit the data collected from wireless sensor networks and IoTs to cloud.

2.3 The Integration of IoT and Cloud

The main reason behind the need for integration of IoT and Cloud technology is developing better solutions in terms of secured and ubiquitous system. The above said features makes the convergence towards integration easier. Out of various domains that gets benefited due to this integration of services, health care industry stand first [10].

The challenges that arise due to the integration of cloud computing and IoT technologies are in terms of security, privacy, heterogeneity, Big data, performance, legal aspects, monitoring, large scale, etc. The various issues to be handled are standardization, the path towards Fog computing, cloud capabilities, SLA enforcement, Big data, energy efficiency, security privacy etc. Fog computing is a decentralized computing extending the concept of cloud computing. It performs data computation at the network edge making it ideal for IoT applications. It acts as a platform in enabling communication between the end users and the services they require. It keeps attention over delay over the network as it is best suitable for latency sensitive applications. It includes features like awareness towards location, edge location, real-time interaction and mobility.

The power of cloud computing and its specific capabilities with regard to its storage, services, applications, energy efficiency, computational capability etc. enhance some of the major of IoT use cases like building automation, smart grids, remote monitoring of patients, smart factory etc. Various Cloud-IoT applications that get benefited because of the above said integration are healthcare, smart cities, smart houses, video surveillance, automotive and smart mobility, smart energy smart grid, smart logistics, environmental monitoring, etc.

Service Models of Cloud – IoT

Cloud IoT integration has led to various new service models described below like SaaS (Sensing as a Service), EaaS (Ethernet as a Service), SAaaS (Sensing and Actuation as a Service), IPMaaS (Identity and Policy Management as a Service), DBaaS (Database as a Service), SEaaS (Sensor Event as a Service), SenaaS (Sensor as a Service), DaaS (Data as a Service).

Sensing as a Service (SaaS)

Delivery of analyzed and processed environmental data, on demand is called SaaS model. The data is collected from sensors in the already existing infrastructure. It also enables to remotely monitor the network assets.

Sensor as a Service (SenaaS)

The model of providing live environmental sensor data on demand, from existing infrastructure, is called SenaaS.

Sensing and Actuation as a Service (SAaaS)

The SAaaS model uses the existing sensors and actuators to assemble and process the environmental data and makes them available to the consumers on demand. The physical sensors and actuators devices are managed by the cloud and it supports QoS requirements in a flexible way.

Data as a Service (DaaS)

Business critical data is made accessible from the cloud to the customers on demand is called DaaS model. It avoids redundancy and cost to accommodate vital data in a single location, to maintain its consistency when accessed by multiple users and to develop software to present the data to the user in the required format.

Database as a Service (DBaaS)

DBaaS model enables users to access, manage, configure and operate database with some set of abstractions, without concerning on exact implementations of the specific database.

Ethernet as a Service (EaaS)

Delivery of Ethernet service across a broadband channel to enable the user to use high bandwidth, fiber optic media, is known as EaaS model. It reduces the cost for Ethernet services to business customers. In EaaS, ensuring best effort services and high bandwidth multimedia services do not create performance problems.

2.3.1 Contributions of Cloud Computing in Internet of Things

Cloud computing services are required for IoT applications mainly because of the availability of huge processing power, security and privacy, removal of barriers while hosting, inter device communication, etc. as shown in Fig. 2.3

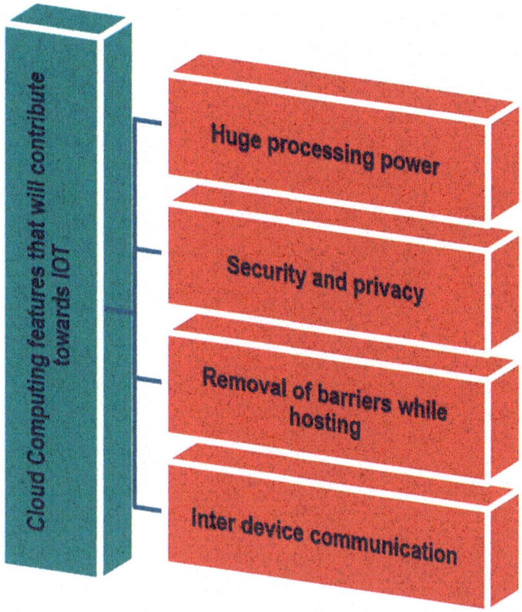

Fig. 2.3 Features of cloud computing contributing to IoT

Cloud computing supports users with huge processing speed. Examples: Dropbox, Google Drive and Amazon S3. Cloud provides security to IoT in terms of prevention, detection and corrective controls with highly sophisticated security algorithms. Authentication and Encryption protocols play a key role in cloud security. Examples: Salesforce, Hubspot, Marketo. Emerging different types of IoT devices requires plug and play model to get connected with the internet. Cloud enables such provision to clients by removing entry barriers for them. Cloud facilitates inter-device communication so that devices communicate with each other without any barrier. Example: Google Cloud. Cloud Capabilities is all about security, since security always remains a major issue with any networking environment. Cloud based IoT has threat of attacks from both sides of cloud and IoT. Threat of attacks of IoT includes attacks related to data integrity, confidentiality, authenticity, etc.

2.3.2 Cloud and IoT: Drivers for Integration

Drivers for integration refers to the motivating factors that drive towards the integration Cloud computing and IoT. These drivers are classified into three major categories namely Communication, Storage and Computation. Cloud streamlines IoT in terms of collection of data, processing of data, integration of things at a lower deployment cost as shown in Fig. 2.4.

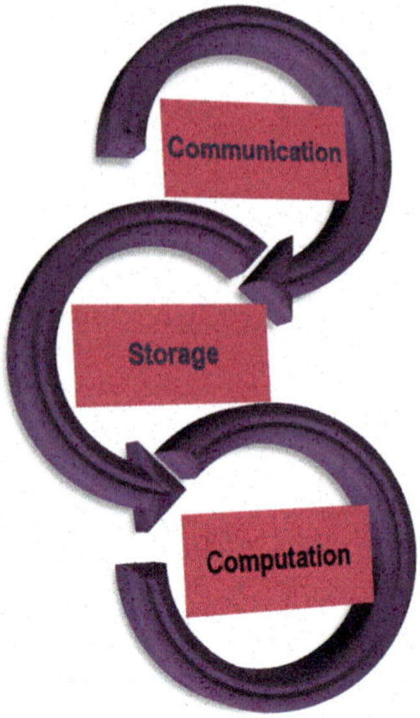

Fig. 2.4 Drivers for integrating cloud computing with IoT

Communication covers data sharing and application sharing drivers. It enables automation towards data collection and data distribution at a lower cost. Cloud environment is known for its customization of platforms that provides a best solution to access any data from anywhere anytime.

Storage is concerned in broad terms of Big Data i.e. Volume, Variety and Velocity because of huge amount of non-structured or semi structured data from various heterogeneous information sources. Cloud provides the facility of unlimited, low cost, on demand storage capacity virtually. Cloud is the best cost effective solution to handle the data produced by IoT which creates trending openings towards data aggregation, data integration and data sharing.

Cloud offers computational facilities to IoT devices that helps complex data processing and data aggregation and supports scalability. IoT devices had theses parameters as main challenges. This category of drivers is concerned about implementation of real time sensor centric scalable applications while saving the energy.

2.3.3 Open Challenges

Atlam et al. [11] has clearly discussed about the various challenges that cloud based IoT integration has faced. The topmost challenges are security and privacy, heterogeneity, big data, performance, legal aspects, monitoring, large scale, etc. as shown in Fig. 2.6.

Security and privacy challenge revolves around fixation of authorization rules and policies in such a way that authorized users have secured access to data. Also it raises other related challenges with respect to physical location of data, SLA (Service

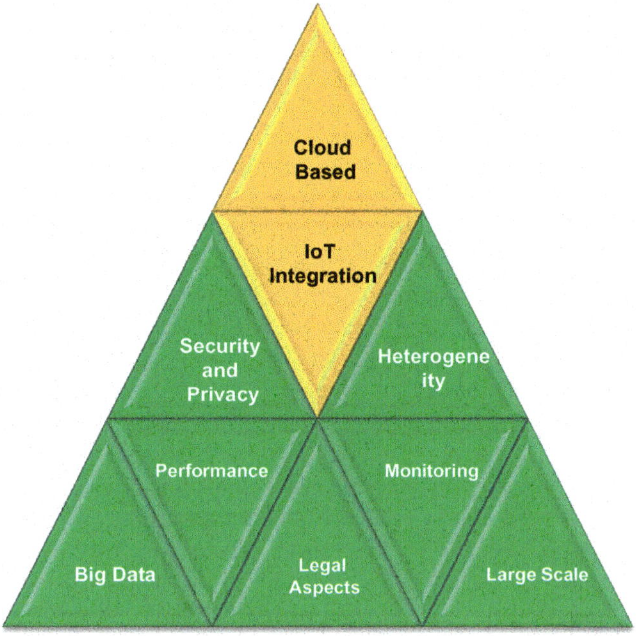

Fig. 2.5 Challenges of cloud based IOT integration

Level Agreement) and trustworthiness of service providers. Multi-tenancy plays a vital challenge among all, because of the threat towards leakage of sensitive information. Other security and privacy related challenges are attacks, SQL injection, session riding, cross site scripting, session hijacking, virtual machine escape etc.

Heterogeneity challenge covers the issues related to extensive heterogeneity of devices, platforms, operating systems, and services that exist and might be used for new or developed applications. Heterogeneity remains a tough challenge because of requirement of resource integration to provide cloud services.

Big data challenge covers the areas of data transportation, data access, data storage and data processing. The beauty of Big Data is its requirement of sources of data from IoT and storage facilities through cloud. This led to the greatest challenge to cloud from the perspective of a perfect data management. It also involves data integrity issues.

Performance is always a challenge irrespective of any integrated domains. Need for sufficient network performance for transferring bulk of data generated by IoT devices towards cloud environment. Real time applications remain sensitive towards the performance. Legal aspects are much concerned about various international regulations (Fig. 2.5).

Monitoring deals with resource management, security and troubleshooting in cloud computing environment. Cloud based IoT integration follows same monitoring policies with few challenges in terms of velocity, volume, and variety characteristics of the IoT.

The last challenge is about analysis and integration of real-world data into IoT environment. This leads to the requirement of communication facility between huge geographically distributed devices in very large scale.

2.3.4 Platforms

Cloud based IoT platforms [12] play a vital role in deciding the efficiency of how smart applications get benefited through cloud based IoT systems. These platforms enable new paradigms like XaaS, SaaS, SAaaS, SEaaS, SenaaS, DBaaS, DaaS, EaaS, IPMaaS, VSaaS as described in Sect. 2.2. These cloud based IoT platforms are found to be more efficient than existing ones based on the parameters like time consumption. Depending upon different category of applications, it is flexible to customize this type of virtual sensing infrastructure. In spite of the perception of requirement of a high-level architecture for a cloud based integrated IoT system, several open source and commercial platforms are available for the same. These platforms provide an API which acts a bridge between heterogeneous IoT devices and Cloud by acting as a middleware. Examples of such platforms and services are IoTCloud, OpenIoT, IoT Toolkit, NimBits, openPicus, Xively, Open Sense, ThingSpeak, CloudPlugs, Carriots, NetLab, Intel IoT Analytics, Synapse IoT Cloud and ClouT.

2.4 Problems of the Existing IOT Cloud Platforms

There are seven major problems with existing cloud based IoT platforms [14] namely Standardization, Heterogeneity, Context awareness, Middleware, IoT node identity, Energy management and Fault tolerance as illustrated in Fig. 2.6.

Context awareness gains importance since it is difficult for any user group to handle data collected from various sensors geographically located in different IoT devices. It gives a clear picture on the data of importance that need to be processed.

Heterogeneity remains a problem with Cloud based IoT system since it enhances complexity in communication between various IoT devices, ending up with network delay. Bandyopadhyay et al. [15] has addressed this issue by suggesting a better solution for effective communication between IoT devices by managing them through addressing, identification and optimization.

Standardization is a major problem with cloud environment since process representation and data representation don't have a standard format. Standardization at application level in a cloud based IoT environment involves interoperability, reducing the barriers for service providers and active users. Cloud based IoT systems need improvements in terms of security standards, communication standards and identification standards.

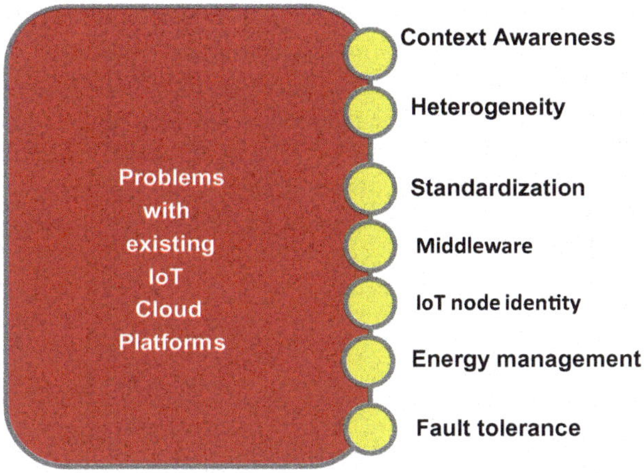

Fig. 2.6 Problems in existing IOT cloud platforms

Cloud based IoT systems require a greater number of middleware for effective data processing. Middleware enables information flow through devices, protocols and applications. It acts as a platform to incorporate the geographically dispersed modules within a tenant. It results in a centralized processing over the whole data set.

IoT node identity is another problem with this existing system as it involves huge number of nodes. Unique identification of devices and data retrieval from them remains a great challenge.

Cloud based IoT systems also face the problem of energy management. Energy management is given much importance in cloud based IoT systems because of the energy consumption by IoT devices and network components in the system.

Fault tolerance remains as a high priority element for any system to function normally in spite technical errors. Possible scenarios that trouble fault tolerance are depleted battery of hardware devices, erroneous value by the sensors, faulty calibration and communication failure. These can be overcome using solar power as an alternative to the battery-operated components and usage of communication protocol to provide seamless connectivity.

2.5 IoT Supporting Technologies and Cloud Service Framework

2.5.1 Cloud Federation in IoT

Celesti et al. [17] has stated the importance of IoT Cloud Federation architecture towards new business opportunities. The main objective of this section is to address the role of evolution of cloud based IoT systems towards federated ecosystems.

IoTaaS (IoT as a Service) model is a service model that provides IoT resources from all the three perspectives of Infrastructure, Platform, and Software. Cloud based IoT system is a type of distributed system which comprises of IoT devices that are interconnected to a cloud infrastructure, platform, or software to enable IoTaaS services. Due to enormous growth of cloud service providers, cloud federations are established by cloud operators to offer flexible services. Added to this, evolution of container virtualization technology is also one strong reason behind the establishment of Cloud Federation.

2.5.2 Virtualization in IoT

Virtualization is defined as a process of hosting one or many Virtual Machines (VMs). These virtual machines can be deployed even in a single physical machine. In that case, these virtual machines are referred as guest operating system and the physical machine is called as host. A Hypervisor co-ordinates and manages all these virtual machines. Hypervisor is also called as Virtual Machine Monitor (VMM). So it is also referred as Hypervisor Virtualization (HVV). For example: Xen, KVM, Virtual Box, Virtual PC, WM-Ware employ HVV.

Virtualization builds services that hide the complexity of underlying hardware or software. This results in offering guaranteed services with reliability, elasticity, scalability, isolation and resource optimization. Cloud based IoT system relies more on Linux Container Virtualization (LCV). This Linux Container Virtualization creates containers for different applications in Linux environment. It is an OS level virtualization technique that helps in creating multiple instances of the typical OS at the user space with sharing of kernel of the host OS. The notable features of LCV are flexibility in setup, configuration, optimization and management of sensing and actuating capabilities. In general, there are two models for containers namely: *Application Containers* and *System Containers*. An Application Container is capable of running only a single application inside the container. System Containers has the flexibility where the container boots an instance of user space. The beauty of this flexibility is simultaneous running of multiple instances of user space inside the container. Each of these instances has its own Init process, process space, file system and network stack. Best examples of containers are Docker, LXC, lmctfy, OpenVZ.

Let's have an overview on why LCV is preferable to HVV. For the applications requiring direct hardware access like access to disks or network devices, in HVV, it gets access through hypervisor's hardware emulation which will drastically reduce their performance. The container helps to eradicate this by using native resources. The applications in the container restricted to its own environment make it more likely to be secure. The startup time to launch a container is much faster than that of a virtual machine. Containers offer direct control over the underlying hardware resources. Linux Kernel provides lot of capabilities to container software to isolate processes from each other.

Load management and fail over of a system relies more on dynamic resource assignment or separation. It focuses on assigning of additional CPUs to heavily loaded VMs or remove CPUs from idle VMs or Containers.

2.5.3 Monolithic IoT Clouds

IoT Clouds are independent by nature. A remote cloud system takes the responsibility of being in charge of collecting, uniform sensing and actuating data coming from heterogeneous IoT devices. Hence IoT devices interact with this cloud system. Containers are used as supportive means to deploy applications in IoT devices. This results in minimal processing and storage tasks being performed in IoT devices and landing up with massive data processing and data analytics jobs at the remote cloud system. This further exploits virtualization technologies to elastically scale up/down storage and processing capabilities. Hence a Cloud based IoT system exploits Linux Container Virtualization technology in IoT devices in order to deploy services and applications in a flexible way. This also extends the possibility to deploy distributed infrastructures, platforms, and applications (IoTaaS) in several distributed containers in a much more flexible way. Thus, cloud based IoT system exploits virtual capabilities and remain responsible for the instantiation, optimization, and management of IoTaaS guaranteeing reliability, scalability, Quality of Service (QoS) and Security. This type of cloud based IoT systems are referred as Monolitich IoT clouds.

2.5.4 Vertical Supply Chain

Next to traditional monolithic clouds is a complex system called as vertical supply chain. Vertical Supply chain system illustrated in Fig. 2.7 is considered to be complex, as it has a constraint of effective coordination system to enable cooperation of different IoT cloud providers. Multi cloud model or cloud bursting model supports each small provider and medium provider to use IoT services of other IoT cloud providers. It is the responsibility of every IoT cloud provider to manage service metering information in order to manage accounting, billing and service placement decisions.

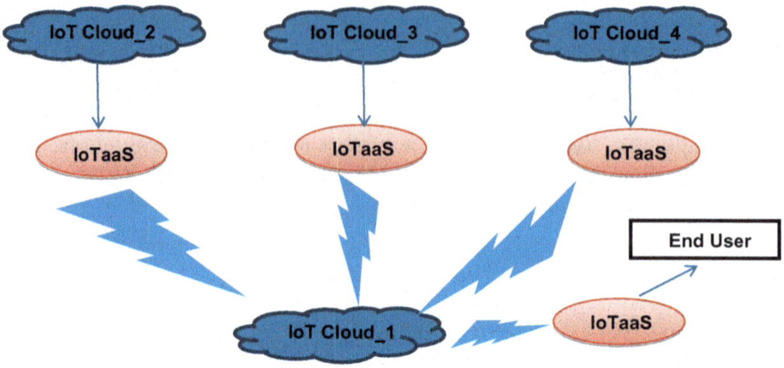

Fig. 2.7 Vertical supply chain scenario

2.5.5 *IoT Cloud Federation*

This section concentrates over the concept of IoT cloud federation. Consider the case study of IoT cloud providers that arrange IoTaaS exploiting the concepts of both Linux Container Virtualization and Hypervisor Virtualization. Virtualization technologies introduce a logical layer between the physical infrastructure and services in order to hide the underlying physical assets. For the case study under consideration, let us assume the usage of both Linux Container Virtualization and Hypervisor Virtualization at the cloud data center and Linux Container Virtualization technique at IoT devices. Private IoT clouds have an in-built nature of owning their own virtualization infrastructures. They have their own virtual machines and containers that are hosted to provide services to their clients.

Cross Cloud Federation permits every IoT Cloud operator to extend the amount of its virtualization resources like increasing the number of virtual machines and containers to support for further storage, computation, sensing, and actuating capabilities to other IoT Clouds. It is the role of the cloud operator to handle the need for any service allocation request of its clients. The IoT Cloud Federation differs from that of IoT Cloud vertical supply chain from the perspective of both political and historical implications. An organization characterized by a joining of partially self-governing entities united by a central government is known as a Federation. Central government has no decision powers to alter the typically independent self-governing status of components in a federation. Hence a group of interconnected IoT cloud providers formed to provide a decentralized sensing and actuating environment driven by constraints and agreements is called as an IoT cloud Federation.

In an IoT cloud Federation environment, an IoT cloud can establish agreements with other IoT clouds to use computing, storage, sensing and actuating capabilities. There are two types of IoT clouds from the perspective of IoT cloud federation namely: Home IoT cloud and Foreign IoT cloud. Home IoT cloud offers additional external sensing and actuating capabilities by forwarding requests to Foreign IoT

Clouds for the purpose of elastically enlarging its IoT infrastructure. Foreign IoT Cloud offers sensing and actuating capabilities to Home IoT Clouds for free or by charge. An IoT Cloud can act as both Home IoT cloud and Foreign IoT cloud simultaneously. The business opportunities created by IoT cloud federation are optimization of resources, power saving and resource provisioning.

2.5.6 Architecture for IoT Cloud Federation

2.5.6.1 Requirements of IoT Cloud Federation

Existing IoT cloud Federation models are static by nature which requires apriori agreements among the cloud parties to be established in the Federation. The important requirements of the IoT Cloud Federation are automatism and scalability, inter-operable resource provisioning and inter-operable security. Automatism and scalability refer to the ability of a Home IoT Cloud to choose its right Foreign IoT cloud that can satisfy its needs. Inter-operable resource provisioning allows the Home IoT Cloud to use the virtualized IoT resources of Foreign IoT Cloud. Inter-operable security allows Home IoT cloud to join the Federation without changing its security policies.

2.5.6.2 Challenges Faced by IoT Cloud Federation

The challenges faced by IoT Cloud Federation are privileged user access, regulatory compliance, data location, data segregation, recovery, investigative support, long-term viability, Quality of Service and inter-operable security. Privileged user access ensures the need for assurance to the sensitive data processed outside the enterprise. Regulatory compliance is a process through which a tenant can verify that an IoT Cloud provider has the necessary external audits and security certifications. The infrastructure complies with regulatory security requirements. Data location is all about the storage of data in cloud, because a cloud provider commits to storing and processing of data in specific jurisdictions and to obey the local privacy requirements on behalf of the client who is totally unaware about the location of data. Data segregation ensures that one tenant's data is fully segregated from another tenant's data. Recovery is required when a disaster occurs, so that an efficient replication and recovery mechanism should be used by the IoT cloud provider to restore data. Investigative support ensures a contractual commitment when a tenant needs to investigate the cloud services. Long-term viability of sensing data is taken care by IoT cloud provider. Quality of Service over IoT services based on Service Level Agreements (SLAs) is effected in spite of IoT devices being typically unreliable. Inter-operable security ensures that a Home IoT Cloud is capable to authenticate itself, gaining the access to the resources provided by the federated Foreign IoT Clouds belonging to the same trust context, without any further identity checks.

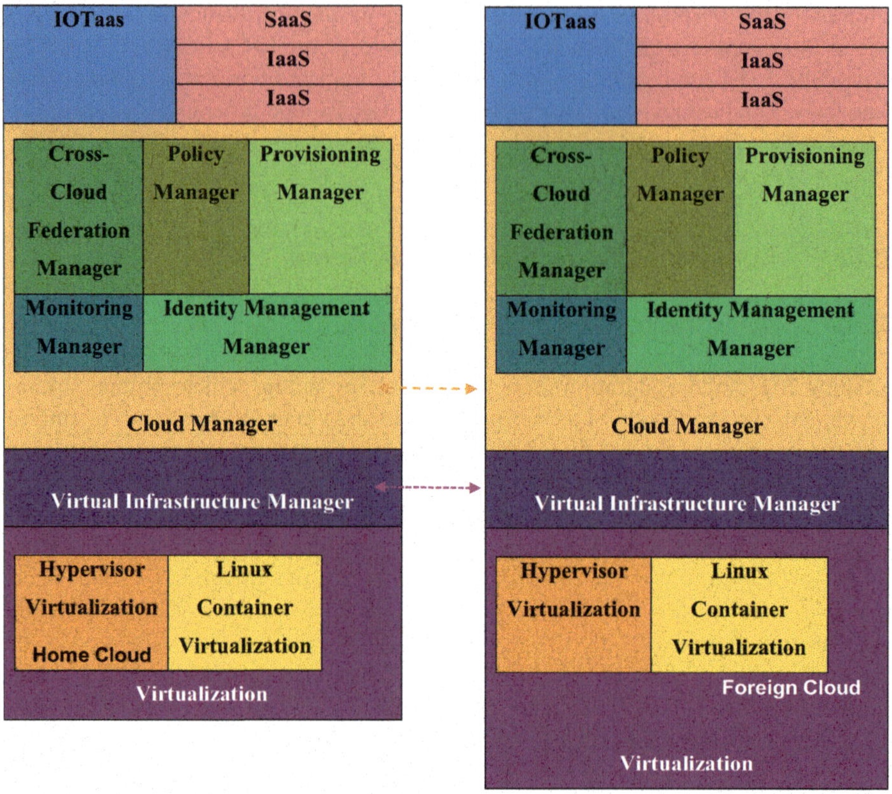

Fig. 2.8 IoT cloud federation architecture

2.5.6.3 IoT Cloud Federation Architecture

The IoT cloud architecture is designed considering inputs from cloud computing systems and IoT requirements. The objective of this architecture is to address the future requirements of IoT cloud federation. Fig. 2.8 represents IoT cloud federation architecture. The bottom most layer is called as virtualization layer, which takes the responsibility of enabling services to physical servers and IoT devices in terms of Linux Container Virtualization technology and Hypervisor Virtualization technology. The middle layer is called as Virtual Infrastructure Manager layer. Hypervisors and container engines are controlled by data centers and IoT devices with the help of middleware deployed on them by this Virtual Infrastructure Manager layer.

The controlling rights can deal with instantiating, setting up, managing, migrating, and destroying virtual machines and containers. Thus, Virtual Infrastructure Manager layer helps data centers to manage virtual machines and containers and helps IoT devices to manage containers. The topmost layer is Cloud Manager layer. It is responsible for providing interfaces for security, contextualization and virtual machine image management. It consists of components that are capable to manage Cross-Cloud Federation, monitoring, Identity Management, access control policies and service provisioning. It also provides IoTaaS in form of IaaS, PaaS, and SaaS.

2.6 Conclusion

This chapter is focused on IoT cloud Paradigm which represents a big leap in the future world of Internet. A number of new applications arising with this combination, called IoT Cloud, open up multidimensional directions for business and research. This chapter addressed the requirements, challenges and drivers to integrate IoT and cloud. It examined the problems in the existing IoT cloud platforms and also discussed the IoT supporting technologies and cloud service framework. It also analyzed how IoT cloud paradigm is evolved into federated systems and its architecture, requirements and implementation challenges. Being the important components of future Internet, IoT and cloud integration will definitely envision the research directions including multi-networking and convergence toward an open service platform for users.

References

1. Takabi H, Joshi JBD (2010) Security and privacy challenges in cloud computing environments. In: IEEE Computer And Reliability Societies, pp 24–31
2. Subashini S, Kavitha V (2010) A survey on security issues in service delivery models of cloud computing. J Netw Comput Appl 1(34):1–11
3. Gubbi J et al (2013) Internet of Things (IoT): a vision, architectural elements, and future directions. Futur Gener Comput Syst 29:1645–1660
4. Suciu G et al (2013) Smart cities built on resilient cloud computing and secure Internet of Things. In: 19th International Conference on Control Systems and Computer Science, Bucharest
5. Zhou J et al (2013) CloudThings: a common architecture for integrating the internet of things with cloud computing. Huazhong University of Science and Technology, Wuhan
6. Soliman M et al (2013) Smart home: integrating Internet of Things with web services and cloud computing. In: IEEE international conference on cloud computing technology and science, Oulu
7. Aazam M et al (2014) Cloud of things: integrating Internet of Things and cloud computing and the issues involved, In: 11th International Bhurban Conference on Applied Sciences & Technology (IBCAST), Islamabad
8. Aazam M et al (2014) Smart gateway based communication for cloud of things. In: IEEE 9th International conference on Intelligent Sensors, Sensor Networks and Information Processing (ISSNIP)symposium on public internet of things, Singapore
9. Aazam M et al (2016) Cloud of things: integration of IoT with cloud computing. Springer, Cham, pp 77–94
10. Ghulam M, Md Mizanur Rahman SK, Alelaiwi A, Alamri A (2017) Smart health solution integrating IoT and cloud: a case study of voice pathology monitoring. IEEE Communications Magazine

11. Atlam HF, Alenezi A, Alharthi A, Walters RJ, Wills GB (2017) Integration of cloud computing with internet of things: challenges and open issues. In: IEEE international conference on Internet of Things (iThings) and IEEE Green Computing and Communications (GreenCom) and IEEE Cyber, Physical and Social Computing (CPSCom) and IEEE Smart Data (SmartData), pp 670–675
12. Le Tu'n A, Quoc HNM, Serrano M, Hauswirth M, Soldatos J, Papaioannou T, Aberer K (2012) Global sensor modeling and constrained application methods enabling cloud-based open space smart services. In: Ubiquitous Intelligence & Computing and 9th international conference on Autonomic & Trusted Computing (UIC/ATC), pp 196–203
13. Irwin D, Sharma N, Shenoy P, Zink M (2010) Towards a virtualized sensing environment. In: International conference on Testbeds and Research Infrastructures, Springer, Berlin, pp 133–142
14. Ray PP (2016) A survey of IoT cloud platforms. Future Comput Inform J 1(1–2):35–46
15. Bandyopadhyay D, Sen J (2011) Internet of things: applications and challenges in technology and standardization. Wirel Pers Commun 58(1):49–69
16. Chang KD, Chen CY, Chen JL., Chao HC (2011) Internet of things and cloud computing for future internet. In: International conference on security-enriched urban computing and smart grid, September, Springer, Berlin, Heidelberg, pp 1–10
17. Celesti A, Fazio M, Giacobbe M, Puliafito A, Villari M (2016) Characterizing cloud federation in IoT. In: 30th IEEE international conference on advanced information networking and applications workshops (WAINA), pp 93–98

Chapter 3
Edge Computing in IoT

Abstract Having understood the inevitable role of the cloud computing in the context of Internet of Things based applications, now it is time to shift our attention to an emerging new paradigm of data processing. Trying to understand the patterns of data produced by the IoT devices right at the edge of the network solves a few significant practical issues involved in uploading all the raw data to the remote cloud server for deriving insights about the phenomenon under study. Edge computing is gaining lot of momentum in the recent days owing to the generously increasing computing and storage power on embedded devices. This chapter looks at how by offloading the computation tasks closer to the producer of the data overcomes the challenges of moving the data to remote cloud server for further analysis. The storage and processing capabilities needed at the edge of the network to realize the edge computing paradigm of computing are also discussed in the chapter.

Keywords Edge devices · Edge computing · Decentralized enterprise data processing · Edge analytics · Edge analytics platforms · Fog computing

Learning Objectives

- To understand the challenges in centralized cloud based data processing for enterprise IoT applications
- To learn the advantages of moving data processing and data analytics closer to the edge of the network
- To study the hardware and software and storage capabilities needed at the edge computing devices

L. S. Jayashree, G. Selvakumar, *Getting Started with Enterprise Internet of Things: Design Approaches and Software Architecture Models*,
https://doi.org/10.1007/978-3-030-30945-9_3

3.1 Introduction

IoT data analytics is normally understood in terms of the following four types:

- Descriptive Analytics – focuses on identifying an event that has occurred in a functional IoT application.
- Diagnostic analytics – tries to explain the reasons and root causes for the occurrence of a given event
- Predictive analytics –focuses on forecasting when a given event is likely to occur in future
- Prescriptive analytics – gives systematic answers to the questions regarding what needs to be done in order to alleviate the event (if it is an undesirable one) or to make it happen again (if it is a desirable one)

In the recent years, apart from the four different types of analytics operations listed above, an exciting new type of analytics called as *Edge Analytics* is gaining popularity and is shown a lot of interest by IoT system developers, researchers and businesses. Edge analytics is bringing about a paradigm shift in the enterprise IoT ecosystem in a steady pace.

In Chap. 2, we have seen the drivers behind the cloud- IoT integration, the issues and challenges in dealing with the IoT data in the centralized cloud servers. The cloud servers, by virtue of their huge storage and computing power, run advanced analytics algorithms to intelligently process the raw data that is generated by the huge number of sensors and smart devices connected to the IoT ecosystem. Data scientists are now thinking of ways to harness the computing power available at the end devices themselves (end devices are nothing but the smart things of an IoT eco system) and with the devices that are used at the edge of the IoT network, such as IoT gateways, network switches etc., These edge devices are typically available closer to the place of generation of data or at one hop away from the devices.

Imagine IoT use cases like structural health monitoring of bridges, on-shore and off-shore oil and gas pipeline monitoring, connected vehicles, agricultural farm land monitoring, smart grids etc. They generally require the IoT devices to be operating continuously in outdoor environments, sometimes in harsh environmental conditions too. In such applications, the cloud server is normally positioned geographically many miles away from the operational site for safety and security reasons. This requires the wireless transmission of raw data over several kilometers to reach the remotely positioned cloud server. When a sudden emergency condition arises, like the failure of a particular process or a machinery element, actions are to be taken immediately without waiting for the instructions from the remote cloud server. In such situations, it does make good sense to take an immediate action against a failure condition, e.g. shutting off a faulty valve in an off shore oil pipeline assembly right away once a failure condition is deduced by the sensor data, instead of sending all these sensor data up to the cloud server and waiting for it to relay its decision all the way back!

Here's another example of an edge computing deployment: An off-shore oil and gas pipeline that has thousands of sensors produce large amounts of data, out of which most of which could be insignificant; it is the data that just confirms to the supervisor that the various components are in good condition and working properly. In such cases, all the sensor data, usually taken at high sampling rate like 1500 samples per second, need not be sent over the network as soon as it is produced; instead, a local computing system can compile and aggregate the data and send only the hourly/ daily summaries to the remote data center or cloud for long-term storage and historical processing. By sending only the summaries/data that is really significant over the network, the total amount of data that traverses the network is hugely reduced, saving a lot of usable network bandwidth.

3.2 Centralized Cloud Model for IoT Data Processing

3.2.1 The Architecture

Figure 3.1 shows a three-tier IoT data processing architecture involving the sensors and actuators at the *bottom tier*, followed by IoT gateways at the *intermediate tier*, physically positioned closer to the devices and finally the cloud server acting as the

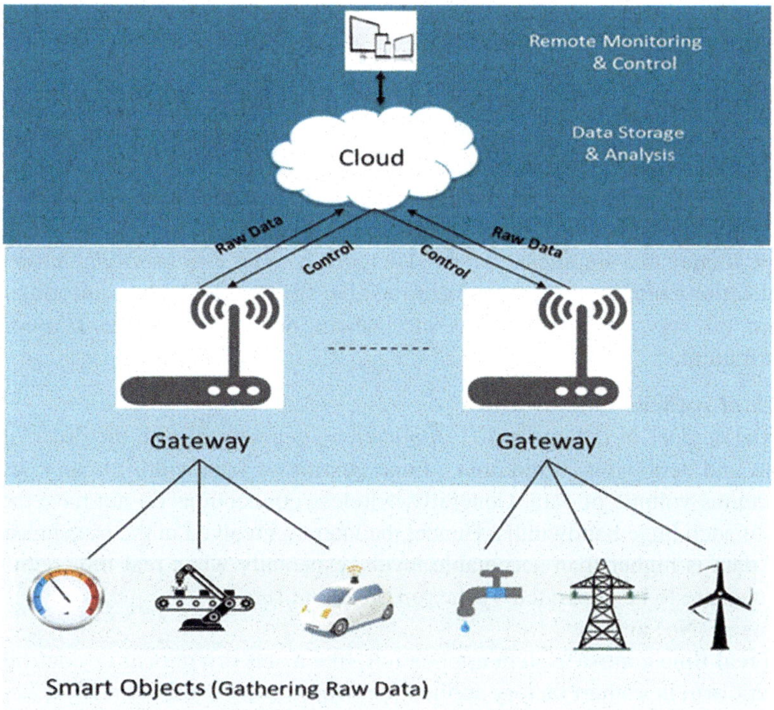

Fig. 3.1 Centralized cloud based IoT data processing architecture

root. The IoT gateways shown in Fig. 3.1 simply forward all the raw data they receive from the sensors and edge IoT devices to the cloud server for further processing. This is because of the fact that, traditionally, the gateways generally do not possess the required intelligence or sophistication to process the data and derive useful insights from the raw data. The gateways perform the roles of simple traffic aggregator in addition to acting as routers for forwarding the data traffic to the cloud. In the reverse direction, it received the control actions or commands from the cloud and forwards it to the appropriate actuating elements.

3.2.2 Challenges in Centralized IoT

The centralized cloud based IoT data processing architecture discussed in the previous section, though simple to implement, has some inherent drawbacks. The process of deriving insights from the data observed by the vast quantity of sensors, when made as the sole responsibility of the cloud server, brings about the following limitations [5]:

- **Intermittent Connections:**
  The raw data that is generated from the sensors need to be carried over the air to the cloud server which is available several kilometers away. Depending on the quality of the wireless connections in the area under consideration, the reliability of data transfer is decided.
  Imagine a situation where the wireless network coverage is less than satisfactory in the geographical area of interest e.g. hilly terrains, offshores etc. Obviously, this will affect the quality of the data transfer leading to intermittent data losses. Hence, when part of the data analytics is performed at the network edge itself and only the processed data or insights are pushed to the cloud, it reduces network latency to a significant extent. This proves to be very useful in outdoor IoT applications running in remote locations like structural health monitoring of off shore oil rigs, chemical plants etc. where network coverage is poor and intermittent.

- **Lack of sufficient bandwidth:**
  As the devices in enterprise IoT applications generate data in the order of peta bytes and zeta bytes, it requires a huge amount of bandwidth to carry such an enormous volume of data. Generally, wireless connections do not have the luxury of such huge bandwidths. Hence, the latency involved in the transmission of raw data is higher than acceptable levels, especially when real time actionable insights are to be generated by the remote cloud server.
- **Delayed (No) actions**
  In a real time control system application, like a self driving car or controlling a robotic arm in a smart factory application, where every millisecond of delay does matter, an action not taken in-time or a delayed action is equivalent to not taking any decision at all.

- **No real-time insights**
  While the processing power keeps increasing day by day, the network speeds are not keeping up at the same pace. As a result, one can imagine the network latency involved in carrying the data containing streaming audio or video to the cloud server (e.g. vision analytics applications, surveillance applications etc.). When the latency involved in transmission of sensor data is higher than acceptable levels, the insights derived by the cloud server do not reflect the real time snapshots of it.
  Hence, enterprise applications prefer to run the machine learning algorithms and big data analytics algorithms directly on the edge devices themselves and reach out to the cloud for long term storage of historic data. Cloud servers are still required to continuously train and adapt the machine learning/deep learning algorithms using the long term historic data.
- **Security & Compliance**

  Data captured by IoT devices may be business-sensitive or confidential by nature. Understandably, transferring the business related operational data over the air makes it vulnerable for security attacks. Considering the risks involved in transferring the business data from the operating premises to the remote cloud server, enterprises would prefer processing the data locally by the edge devices. Many enterprises have started to think about using private cloud in conjunction with edge computing to alleviate the risks involved in third-party interception of private business data. With edge computing in place, businesses can make sure that the business related sensitive data is preprocessed locally and only privacy compliant data flow to the cloud server for further analysis.

3.3 Shifting the Intelligence to the Edge

3.3.1 What Is Edge Computing?

The solution to the problems discussed in Sect. 3.2 with regard to the centralized cloud based data processing is the *decentralized data processing* architecture [5] called as *Edge Computing*. In an edge computing framework, instead of allowing all the raw data generated from the edge devices flow to the cloud server, they are processed locally at the edge gateways and only selected data or the insights alone flow to the cloud server.

In the edge computing model, the IoT gateways, in addition to performing the role of routers to forward the data to the cloud, also store the data and perform some intelligent processing on the data received from the devices. Edge computing allows us to do pre-processing or filtering of the data closer to the location where the data is being created. Thus, all those data that falls within the normal limits can be ignored or stored in a low cost storage and any faulty or abnormal conditions can be immediately acted upon in near real-time.

Edge computing can hence be understood as the technique of data acquisition, processing and analysis of the collected data close the source of the data, at a device like an IoT gateway or a network switch or some other custom built device with sufficient computing power. This enables *real time* and in-situ analysis of the huge data collected from various sensors and IoT devices.

3.3.2 The Need for Edge Analytics

IoT Edge Analytics is typically applicable for outdoor IoT applications involving systems like oil rigs, mines, factories etc. which operate in low bandwidth, low latency environments. Edge analytics could apply not just to sensor data but also to richer forms of data such as voice and video analytics. Given the present scenario of largely connected devices and the projected scenario of even higher proliferation of smart devices in the upcoming years which generate massive volumes of data - in the order of peta bytes and zetta bytes, enterprises have started to invest their time and money to leverage the huge amount of data to gain better business insights. Such intelligent insights derived as a result of advanced IoT data analytics techniques would help businesses to take informed decisions that would improve their overall business value and revenues.

In a typical decentralized edge computing application, different computing modules can be deployed at different elements of the data processing architecture shown in Fig. 3.2. For instance, an analytics engine might be running in the cloud for performing historical data processing on the long term data archives. A dash board module provides an interface for querying and visualization. Training of the machine learning algorithm may be done at the edge gateways while the actual execution may happen at the edge devices. The various rules governing the interaction and communication among the various modules, the visibility constraint, security checks etc. may be clearly defined in the business logic.

3.3.3 Edge Computing: Sample Business Use Cases

Edge computing is a distributed architecture in which the raw data is processed at the periphery of the network, as close to the source of the data as possible. Companies like Cisco, Intel and others were early proponents of edge computing by positioning their gateways as edge devices. Now, a new segment of the market is developing driven by vendors like IBM, Cisco, Dell, GE and others. These vendors are positioning their servers as edge devices by adding additional storage, computing power and analytics capabilities.

Understanding the fact that tens of billions of smart things are generating massive volumes of data, industries have to do significant investments in the coming years to handle the data to derive proper business insights. Advanced big data

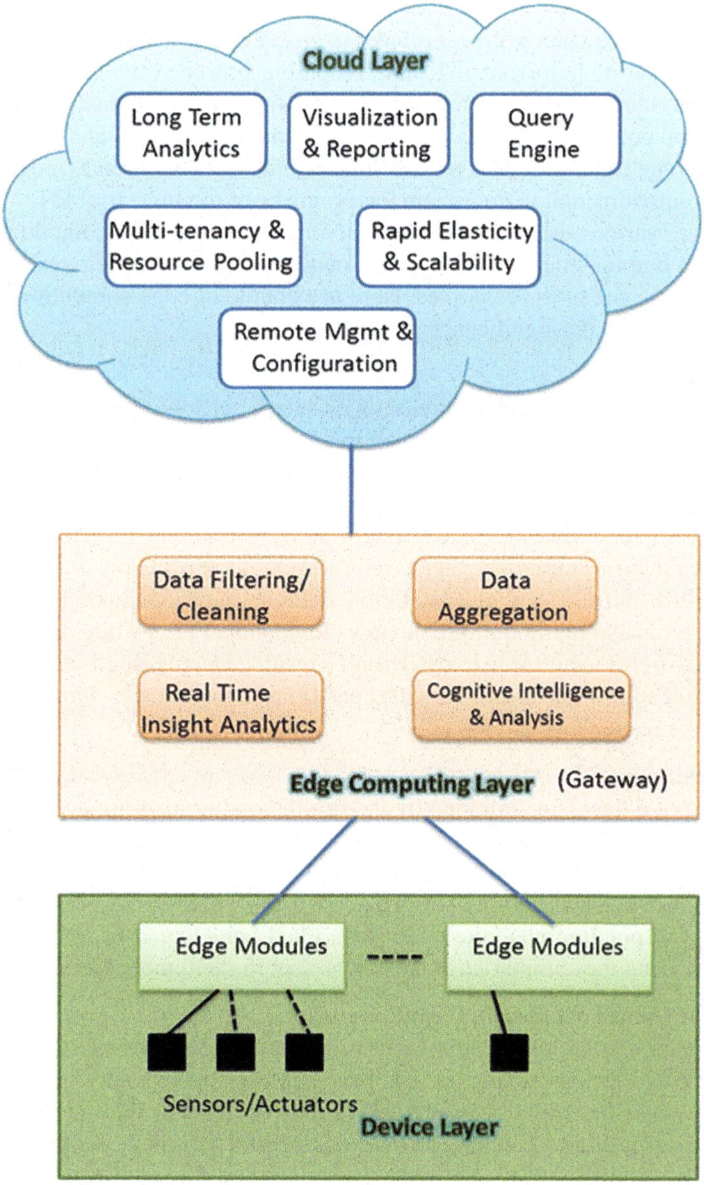

Fig. 3.2 The decentralized edge computing architecture for IoT data processing

analytics techniques and advanced machine learning algorithms are increasingly being used in business operations. This helps businesses and enterprises to gain better asset performance, reduce unplanned downtime, reduce maintenance costs, reduce energy consumption and predict failures in advance. Better business models can be worked out by tapping the hidden value of the operational data.

Cloud computing has been heavily used by industries over the past few decades for its compute and storage power offered to business applications as services. With the introduction of Industrial IoT, the computing power available with the cloud plays a vital role in effectively handling the massive amount of data generated from the industrial equipments and machinery. Nevertheless, as more and more computing and storage capabilities are packed into edge devices themselves, edge computing will be instrumental in delivering the promises of the Industrial IoT.

There are various use cases in different verticals where edge computing plays a vital role in helping enterprises provide a better experience to their customers. The following are some of the examples. Here is a couple of edge computing examples to help understand the significance of edge computing.

Autonomous Vehicles
The self driving cars, with hundreds of on-board sensors, generate several terra bytes of data every day. Needless to mention, it is impractical to send all those to the cloud for storage or analytics. Most of these data, like a traffic signal approaching or a dog crossing the road, are only transient in nature and significant for a very short term. In such use cases, what matter more is how quick a decision is made. The driving decisions are to be taken right away and the actuators are to be effected with ultra-low latency. Any non-negligible delay in decision making and actuation (applying break, stopping the vehicle on a closed signal etc.) while driving through busy urban streets would lead to catastrophic results. Here is where edge computing plays a vital role in ensuring the safe operation of the vehicle, thus ensuring the safety of the passengers and the public.

Fleet Monitoring
The health of a fleet is determined by the health conditions of its several key functional elements, like its wheels, battery, brakes etc. These individual elements could be monitored regularly in order to do proactive maintenance that will improve the uptime of the fleet and optimal performance of the vehicle. The health monitoring and the corresponding analytics of an individual vehicle can be done by an edge device itself and the summaries alone can be sent to the remote cloud server.

Structural Health Monitoring Applications:
In a typical civil structure health monitoring application, sensing instruments like strain gauges, accelerometers, moisture sensors etc. are typically instrumented at key locations of the structure being monitored. These sensors send their gathered data to an on-site edge computing device which performs operations like data acquisition, data cleaning, signal conditioning etc. Besides, the intelligent sensor fusion module running in the edge computing device may run an ensemble of machine learning algorithms for intelligent aggregation of multi modal sensor data to diagnose the type of structural failure. Intelligent post processing of aggregated sensor data using a combination of statistical, machine learning and fuzzy inference techniques to predict the likely course of the damage and to predict the severity of

imminent failures (damage prognosis). Generates diagnostic and prognostic reports and charts in the prescribed format assist structural engineers to make informed decisions on the repair and retrofitting strategies. In a typical smart city application, reports generated from several such *in-situ* edge devices across various locations of the city send the reports and insights generated to the common cloud server managed by a single administrative authority.

3.4 The Edge Computing Architecture

In a centralized cloud based IoT architecture, the entire raw data produced from smart devices and sensors flow to the cloud whereas in an edge computing architecture, the data processing is completely decentralized and is done closer to the source of the data and only the pre-processed data and insights drawn from the collected data flow to the cloud as depicted in Fig. 3.2.

Edge computing architecture is distributed by nature. The architecture consists of devices of three types based on their functionality. They are:

- Edge Gateways
- Edge Devices, and
- Edge Sensors and Actuators

Edge Sensors and Actuators are special purpose devices either embedded in edge devices or connected to edge gateways, typically through Personal Area Networking (PAN) standards like low energy Bluetooth, Zigbee etc. or Local Area Networking (LAN) standards like Ethernet or WiFi and other advanced wireless communication standards as discussed in Chap. 1.

Edge Devices are generally battery powered. They are either special purpose devices or general purpose devices which are capable of running full-scale operating systems. Smart phones running Android or iOS, industrial machines, industrial controllers such as SCADA systems and sensors are good examples for such devices.

Edge gateways are similar to edge devices but they generally enjoy unconstrained power supply, more computing power and storage. They sit in between the cloud server and the edge devices.

Edge devices and edge gateways are good proponents to run computational intelligent techniques to process the data collected from edge sensors; they are able to take local decisions and send appropriate commands to actuators. They contact the cloud server through Local Area Networking standards like Ethernet, WiFi etc. or Wide Area Networking standards like 3G/4G, WiFi, LoRA etc. depending on the distance involved, nature of the location, availability of networking services etc.

3.5 Capabilities Needed at the Edge Devices

This section focuses on the capabilities needed at the edge devices so that it fulfills its stated requirements without jeopardizing the performance when compared to its centralized cloud model counterpart. Some of these devices are as compact as smart phones, some are wall mountable, some are rack mountable etc. Depending on its point-of-presence, space and the computing power needs of the particular use case, a particular type of edge device or edge gateway is chosen. The edge computing devices should be compact in size and at the same time rugged enough for outdoor and harsh environmental operations. For example, they should be capable of withstanding shocks, vibrations, high ambient temperature and pressure situations required by applications like off- shore oil and gas pipeline monitoring, structural integrity monitoring of bridges etc. The devices should be capable of running adequate security algorithms as securing these devices is another vital issue so that they can withstand different types of data breaching attacks.

3.5.1 Design Principles for Edge Devices

Some of the key factors that make edge computing realizable and helping industries to turn the huge volumes of data into intelligent and actionable insights right at the network edge are:

- availability of higher computing power and storage for lesser cost
- cost of development and form factor of the embedded devices continue to drop.
- ever growing volume of data from the world around us
- availability of advanced machine learning and data analytics techniques

Besides being the need to be compact and ruggedness for out-door, harsh environmental conditions, some of the key design principles to be borne in mind while designing edge devices can be summarized as:

- **Security:**
  Security of the billions of edge devices operating at outdoor environments is at stake. When the workload from the cloud is going to be off-loaded to the on-site edge devices, there is a need for these devices to be tamper-proof, otherwise they can be compromised and valuable enterprise data can be compromised.
- **Remote management and configurability:**
  The edge devices should be capable of being managed and reconfigured from the remote cloud server. Assuming that today we use a particular machine learning algorithm in the edge, say for instance, to classify the failure risk of a particular machine element in an Industrial IoT application, and in future we decide to change a better version of the classification algorithm, then we just need to reprogram the edge device over-the-air. And since so many edge devices are

deployed in several geographical regions in a large scale IoT application, each of these devices can be reconfigured in one-go from the remote cloud server.

- **Cross platform operation:**
  Edge device should support multiple platforms like Windows, Linux, Android etc.
- **Scalability:**
  Seamless integration of advanced capabilities on to the edge should be made possible without causing any disruption or degradation to the current functioning.

3.5.2 The Hardware Enablers for Edge Devices

What are hardware capabilities needed at an edge device to fulfill its requirements? More and more compact and yet highly powerful hardware are being released in the market as the hardware enablers for the edge devices. From the advanced SoCs (System-on-Chip) to GPUs (Graphic Processing Units), from TPUs (Tensor Processing Units) to fully converged hardware, very powerful hardware capabilities are on offer for the IoT application developers, that are capable of running deep neural networks and advanced analytics algorithms. In addition, a plethora of networking standards and storage solutions are available in the market. Besides, micro data centers are also on the rise which are suitable for large scale enterprise applications which need to store their operational data for several days or months together at the point of presence.

As millions of devices are envisaged to participate in the enterprise IoT ecosystem, wireless connectivity options should also be equally scalable. Internet of Things is already identified as the main use case of the upcoming 5G wireless network standard. In addition, cutting edge networking technologies like Network Virtualization, Software Defined Networks are also believed to play a major role in enterprise IoT use cases.

As there is a broad range of processors available for use with edge devices, the selection criteria is based on how much of the computing power is needed at the edge for the intended application and how much of energy it can afford to spend, especially in outdoor applications that are of unattended nature.

In the Intel family of processors, Xeon D, is best suited to edge devices, owing to the fact that it is a 16 core processor and requires only 45 watts of power, while Xeon E5 is an 8 core processor requiring 135 watts of power with 3.8 GHz capability and Xeon E3 is a 4 core processor which requires 80 watts of power.

The popular microcontroller options available for edge devices are ARM Cortex family of microcontrollers, Intel Quark etc. Intel Quark range of controllers provide computing power in the range of 32–400 MHz with the power requirement of 25 mwatts to 2.2 watts. When compared to Quark, ARM Cortex range of microcontrollers provide much higher computing power where ARM Cortex V8 stands out with 2.5 GHz computing power at the cost of a little higher than 2 watts of power requirement. Hence, low compute applications may use Quark controllers and high compute applications may use ARM cortex.

Given the fact that advanced machine learning algorithms and deep neural networks do lot of heavy and repeated mathematical computations and their learning algorithms train on massive data sets which makes them to run continuously for hours or days together, the CPU s will heat too much that cooling itself requires lot of power. This necessitates specialized accelerators like GPUs, FPGAs or TPUs to run such heavy algorithms, when CPUs alone cannot meet the heavy computing requirements and heat up a lot.

GPUs are much faster in running deep neural networks and advanced machine learning algorithms when compared to CPUs. Training the deep neural networks requires lot of data and lot of computing power in parallel; nevertheless, GPUs suffer during the execution of the algorithms and they are not as fast as CPUs.

Although Graphics Processing Units (GPUs) and Central Processing Units (CPUs) are the popular choices for deep learning execution today, Field Programmable Gate Arrays (FPGAs), Application Specific Integrated Chips (ASICs), and System-on-Chip (SoC) accelerators are also becoming potential choices for running real time analytics applications. Hardware accelerators like GPUs, ASICs, FPGAs, and even SoCs have their own advantages and design trade-offs.

Field Programmable Gate Arrays (FPGA)

One of the main advantages of FPGAs is its reprogrammability. That means the same hardware will be used for running different algorithms; invest on them once and tomorrow when the business model or changes, simply reprogram them to get the required functionality. In the face of rapidly growing use cases and constantly evolving machine learning algorithms, FPGAs offer the required flexibility in reprogramming the edge device as and when necessary, after its deployment in an end to end enterprise use case.

When it comes to the computing power of the FPGAs, they offer 1500 GFLOPS and yet they are less energy hungry. Less power consumption is another aspect where FPGAs outperform CPUs and GPUs. FPGAs are increasingly being used nowadays in applications requiring real time AI. Intel's self driving cars, search engines like Bing, Baidu etc. are some of the examples that use FPGAs for their operation. They have lower latency than CPUs and GPUs in terms of execution speed.

ASICs and Tensor Processing Units (TPU)

Tensor Processor Unit (TPU) is an example of Google's own ASIC hardware. FPGAs are obviously better than GPUs in terms of compute speed, they too have certain limitations. However, TPUs are orders of magnitude times faster. ASICs are orders of magnitude faster than GPUs and FPGAs in running deep neural networks and consume less power. Google uses it for voice based command operations, which are to be executed in real time and results to be fetched in real time too. They are very costly and not reprogrammable. Google, Facebook etc. use this to run complex machine learning algorithms on smart phones and wearable devices.

Fig. 3.3 Converged gateways with one unit form factor

Converged Gateways

A converged gateway, like the one shown in Fig 3.3, is a hardware offering that brings the power of cloud on the edge device. It includes compute, storage, network and virtualization all integrated together in the same hardware package. They should be compact in size and be designed to sustain harsh environmental conditions. Workstation class GPUs like Intel Xeon E3 or Xeon D are good candidates for use with converged servers for gateways. Such devices are expected to have a huge storage capacity of up to 4 TB, should offer plug-and-play operation and should be able to connect to a networking infrastructure offering a bandwidth of several tens of Giga bits per second).

By virtue of its features in terms of its size, computing power, storage capacity etc., converged servers are becoming more and more relevant to act as a powerful edge device.

3.5.3 The Edge Software Stack

As the performance of the edge analytics device depends on several factors with regard to data collection, data preprocessing, learning model selection, deployment and fine tuning of the learning models etc., the processing and storage capacities of the edge devices play a vital role. Apart from the microprocessors, microcontrollers, sensors and memory, the edge software stack is continuously being provided on general purpose computing systems. IBM, Microsoft, Cisco, Amazon, GE are some of the major players providing the software platform for edge analytics. Edge analytics devices require some special capabilities as developing edge analytic model is not an easy task. It involves developing the data analytics model, deploying the model on the edge device and running it. More details of the edge computing platforms can be found in Sect. 4.6.

3.5.4 The Complete Infrastructure Review: From the Device to the Cloud

In order to run vision analytics and advanced signal processing algorithms required by the current Enterprise IoT use cases, powerful microcontrollers like Intel Quark, ARM Cortex etc. are used to build smart devices. Apart from the microcontrollers,

System-on-Chip (SoC) built with, say, 64 bit ARM Cortex V8, also called as Cavium, brings in the same power as a Xeon processor to the device. These days, very powerful SoCs are built with the help of Intel Quark processors and ARM cortex family of microcontrollers. For example, SoCs for movement tracking and gesture recognition are available in the size of a shirt button. Similarly, brain implantable video SoCs help blind people to see, and sound SoCs help deaf and dumb people to talk and listen. These are only some of the examples and the future is yet to see more.

In situations where typical edge devices do not offer the required computing capability, server class devices can be used in applications which require high sampling rate. For example, in a structural health monitoring application, the accelerometers and strain gauges are programmed to take 1500 samples per second when a slight tremor or other events of emergency is sensed. The server class devices have very high compute and storage capabilities and are useful for performing real time video analytics with streaming data (Fig. 3.4).

Apart from gateways and servers, micro data centers are also used in large scale enterprise applications, when the edge processing capability offered by a single server is not sufficient. They consist of tens of high performance processors mounted on a 15 unit to 30 unit rack. They are modular and hence can be deployed in several indoor and outdoor IoT applications and are designed to be rugged for use in vulnerable operating conditions. A sample snapshot of the features of the different component parts of the complete infrastructure, from the simple end device to the powerful cloud server, is depicted in Fig 3.4.

3.6 The Edge Computing Platforms

The following are some of the popular edge computing platforms available in the market. These players already have their presence strongly in the cloud and they have released their edge counterparts. For instance, Amazon has released AWS Green grass as the edge counterpart of its AWS. Similarly, IBM has released Watson with lot of cognitive analytics capabilities. Apache Edgent is an open source offering of edge computing platform. Open whisk and Open fog are some of the other open source offerings in the edge computing ecosystem. Cisco has come up with IOx edge computing platform and allows network devices like switches or routers as edge devices and allows a secure connectivity through its internetworking operating system, IOS.

Whatever provisions are already there in the cloud like data analytics, streaming analytics, advanced machine learning, device integration etc., they are also made available at the edge, perhaps with less carbon foot print. But the important requirement is that, *consistency* should be maintained between the cloud and the edge in terms of their programming model, so that the data analytics or other data aggregation modules already developed for cloud can be moved down to the edge with little tweaking like modifying a few lines of code.

When it comes to any big data analytics problem, the real challenge lies because of the *volume, velocity* and *veracity* of the data. When it comes to IoT data analytics,

Microcontrollers	SoC	Gateway	Server	Micro Data Centre

ARM Cortex Boards running Tensor Flow Lite	**System-on-Chip**	**Intel Atom / i5 dual-core**	**Intel E5-26xx V4 family**	
• set of core operators, both quantized and float • Flat Buffers-based model file format • On-device interpreter with kernels • Smaller in size	• Cell-based Switch Fabrics • Networking Interfaces (Interlaken, SPI-4, CSIX, etc…) • Memory Interfaces (ZBT, QDR, SDRAM, FCRAM, DDR2, DDR3) • 10G & 40G router Fabric Chipset	• 1.46 / 1.9 GHz • On-board GPU • 4-8 GB RAM • 32 – 64 GB SSD • 1U / 2U form factor • Rugged for harsh edge	• 64 to 176 cores • 32 GB to 12 TB RAM • 9.6 – 460 TB storage • 12M + IOPS, 60GB/s transfer rate • 2U (H 3.5" x W 17.25" x L 36.5") • Rugged for harsh edge	• 10s of processors in a single 19 in 15U to 30U rack • Rapidly deployable indoor, outdoor • Designed to withstand in rugged, high risk zones

Fig. 3.4 The end- to- end computing infrastructure

in addition to the above well known challenges, what adds more to the complexity is the fact that the data coming from on-site operational devices, temperature monitoring devices, fire alarms etc. alone are not sufficient to derive proper business insights. They have to be integrated with enterprise wide IT infrastructure data, such as those coming from different departments like HR, finance, CRM, supply chain etc. to draw better business insights out of the Enterprise IoT application. For instance, in a home automation system, replacing the batteries of a thermostat, a vendor requires the service level agreement of the customer with the enterprise, in addition to the battery status data and other meta data of the device etc. But unfortunately the traditional analytics tools and technologies are not designed to handle and work on such combined data sets. Besides, cleaning the data generated by the on-premise edge devices from noisy, corrupt and faulty readings is another major challenge.

3.6.1 Edge Computing Using Microsoft Azure IoT Edge

Microsoft was one of the first to offer an end-to-end IoT platform in the public cloud. Azure IoT Edge is designed as a modular and extensible edge counterpart of Microsoft Azure's cloud services. As discussed in previous sections, the edge devices are often deployed in remote outdoor environments which are typically not easily accessible and sometimes harsh too. Owing to this fact, once they are commissioned, they need to be managed only from the remote cloud server and all further upgrades and maintenance should be done only over-the-air. These upgrades and offloading of tasks could be done either online or offline. If the network connectivity is poor to accept a new upgrade, then they are off loaded into the device once it regains connectivity.

The architecture of Azure IoT is given in Fig. 3.5. Azure IoT Edge seamlessly manages the interaction between devices and public cloud. It does all the necessary plumbing involved in authentication and communication among local devices.

The Components of Azure Architecture
Devices

The end devices are those available on the actual premises of operation. They comprise of sensors and actuators to monitor a phenomenon and to act upon a phenomenon. In an edge computing scenario, these devices talk to the cloud through the edge computing layer. Each end device has a module and all such modules of the various devices available on-site for the given IoT use case, are registered with the IoT hub, which is part of the Azure architecture. The Azure IoT hub does the required data formatting and translations suitable for these devices. The module of each device has a module instance deployed and managed by the edge run time, in the form of a container. The details of modules are explained in the following section.

Modules

The Azure services are realized in terms of what are called as *modules,* the means by which a true edge computing and edge analytics capability are delivered to the edge devices. Each module defines a work load for the device to perform a well-defined action, for instance a data filtering operation, running an analytics algorithm etc., with each module adding a new capability to the device. It is *containerized* so

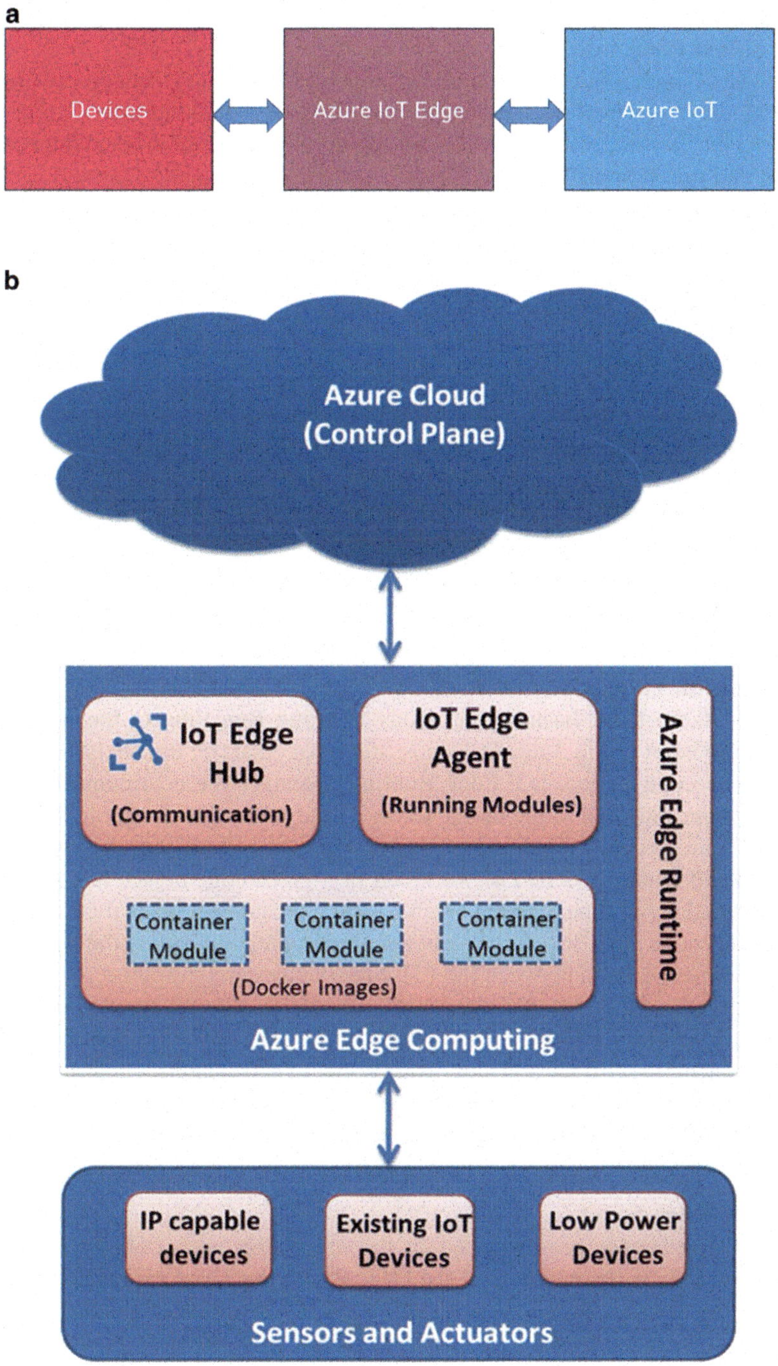

Fig. 3.5 (**a**, **b**) The microsoft azure IoT edge computing architecture

that it becomes portable and can be developed at the cloud and deployed on the device as and when needed.

A chain of such modules together forms an end-to-end IoT data processing scenario. Modules are implemented as Docker Containers making it easy to package them together as one comprehensive service. It allows one to implement a custom module and run it on different platforms.

In Azure platform, a *module image* is the software package that defines a module and when it is actually made to run on an edge device by the *edge run time*, it is called as *module instance*. Each module instance has a *module identity* that is stored on an *IoT Hub*. The module identity incorporates the required security credentials for the module instance and is verifiable at the cloud. Modules can be developed using different languages like C, Python, C#, Node.js etc.

Module Twins

Module images, the direct representations of the IoT devices, they have their digital twins available in the cloud to manage and configure the devices. The module instance is associated with its corresponding digital twin using the module identity. The twin is used to read the status of the device and to set the desired properties to the on-site devices from the remote cloud server. The querying of the device data based on their location, type of data being sensed, model and make of the device etc. is done with the help of the metadata stored in the digital twins of the devices.

IoT Edge Run Time

Microsoft Azure Edge basically provides an Edge Run time to the IoT devices which is the heart of the Azure IoT ecosystem. An edge run time gets deployed on each on-site edge device. IoT Edge Runtime manages the communication to the devices on one side and to the cloud server on the other side. It is containerized so that it becomes portable and can be developed at the cloud and deployed on the device as and when needed. The workload of a given edge device is installed and updated by edge run time. It can be viewed as a management plane that manages all the modules of an edge device. It facilitates communication among the modules and also the communication between the IoT edge devices and the cloud.

The edge run time provides a means for the devices to securely connect to the Internet and manage data when they are offline. Each edge device establishes a secure connection with the IoT hub using some of the established security frameworks like Public Key Infrastructure. The edge run time is analogous to the container management framework like Kubernetes. Because of this, a Kubernetes connector has been built by Microsoft for Azure IoT Hub based on Virtual Kubelet.

Azure IoT Edge Agent

Whenever an edge device is powered on, the Azure edge agent bootstraps itself and runs as the very first component of the Edge Run time. The Azure edge agent then performs the required deployment downloads of the module images onto the edge devices based on the configuration already defined for the edge device. It makes sure that all the module images's configurations are matching with the original definition of the edge device. If there is a change in module definition or when a new module is added, it immediately pulls the required container images and executes them according to the predefined state and configuration information of the device.

Azure IoT Edge Hub

As we have seen in the earlier sections, the device's digital twin mimics the device in the cloud. In the same way, the IoT hub has its counterpart in the cloud, called Edge hub. A module that represents an end device gets authenticated with the local IoT hub by means of the authentication services exposed by the IoT hub to the local end devices. Subsequently, using the communication services offered by the IoT hub, the device can send its sensed data to the hub using the standard communication protocols like MQTT. In this way, the edge hub serves the job of communication broker for the on-site end devices.

In short, modules are placed close to the devices while Edge Agent and Edge Hub are close to the control plane of the cloud. The runtime manages and orchestrates the workflow involved in connecting the ends of the spectrum.

If you carefully notice, you can understand that the Edge Runtime is very similar to a container management platform like Swarm or Kubernetes. Taking advantage of this design, Microsoft has built a Kubernetes connector for Azure IoT Hub, which is based on Virtual Kubelet.

IoT Edge Hub

The Edge Run time together with the IoT hub is used to securely connect, monitor and manage billions of devices to develop IoT applications. The IoT hub provides the full control over a device to configure a workflow, target a particular device to deploy the workflow and monitor the device. Each module/ device has a module twin/device twin in the hub which allows to configure the module.

3.7 Edge vs. Fog Computing

And finally, let us define a very close term associated with edge computing. While edge computing is concerned about moving computing and intelligence closer to generation of data, fog computing focuses on providing the network connectivity and the required network infrastructure for the edge – cloud interplay. The fog layer sits in between the edge layer and the cloud layer and usually it is geographically away from the businesses operating premises and also not in the business's control. It typically refers to modular data centers and the network infrastructure owned by a service provider or a telecom operator, which are leased or rented by the businesses. The processing and communication elements available at the fog layer are called as fog nodes. The decision on which tasks to be performed at the edge layer and which should be uploaded to the fog nodes is the discretion of the developer and the nature of the use case.

It was Cisco that introduced this term in 2014 as a standard that defines how edge computing needs to function. The reference architecture for fog computing called as the *OpenFog Consortium*, is developed by Cisco playing the lead role and backed by organizations like Intel, Microsoft, Dell EMC and Universities like Princeton and Purdue.

3.8 Cognitive Edge Computing for Health Care: The Role of SDN in IoT Edge: Cloud Alliance

The Internet of Things (IOT) faces continuous uplift in healthcare industry as usage of wearable health and fitness monitoring devices are on continuous rise and thereby contributing to our healthy living and longevity as well. The broad range of wearable and implantable health and well monitoring devices leads to connected health care solutions and ambient assisted living environments which keeps increasing the volume of healthcare traffic in the network. The data generated by these devices has to be moved to the cloud for storage, further processing and computation. Relaying such huge amount data to the centralized cloud may lead to network congestion. Additionally, it would result in latency issues and affect desired Quality of Service (QoS) and Quality of Experience (QoE) measures for healthcare applications.

The challenges of the network with respect to dealing with health care traffic are:

- Edge devices are mobile
- Classification of delay sensitive and low priority data and prioritizing emergency data
- User privacy and confidentiality issues
- Overloading of resources on edge devices may lead to high energy consumption.

If there is a shortage of resources on edge nodes, majority of the data has to be relayed to the cloud. All these require huge number of communication between the network edge and the cloud. But the underlying network is responsible for providing low latency for applications. The traditional network may act as a bottleneck to address the above as it depends on standard protocols and architecture. So an inefficient network can lead to high latency and network congestion. Thus, better data transmission mechanism along with efficient and flexible network infrastructure is required which can be achieved by Software Defined Networking (SDN) technology.

SDN is a programmable, scalable, flexible, vendor-independent and reconfigurable network architecture which is required to handle huge data and to improve performance by minimizing latency. It separates control plane from data plane which reduces network congestion and complexity. The data plane performs only forwarding functions instructed by the SDN controller in the control plane. The control plane decides all the forwarding decisions according to the control logic in the SDN controller. The control logic can be programmed and reconfigured according to different environments. Thus this property of SDN is inculcated in the proposed edge cloud interplay framework to optimize bandwidth and latency.

The SDN controller implements traffic rerouting to transmit the traffic either from cloud to edge (forward offloading) or from edge to cloud (reverse offloading) depending on the availability of resources on them. It reduces computational cost and network latency and finally enhances QoS and QoE level of healthcare services. Thus SDN is one of the promising networking technologies in the multi-edge cloud environment.

3.9 Conclusion

As the Internet of Things space is continuously witnessing a variety of different use cases, each with different QoS and traffic handling requirements, the need for edge computing is on the rise.

Even though edge computing replicates most of the cloud services, by no means it can replace cloud, but it indeed complements it, thus helping businesses gain better edge over its competitors. Because of the distributed nature of edge computing as opposed to the centralized scheme of its cloud computing counterpart, it has greater potential to deliver improved services in use cases involving a huge amount of data to be analyzed and those requiring real time actions. It is believed that edge computing is the key to leverage the complete potential of IoT but it calls for more serious research in providing advanced data analytics services like cognitive analytics, deep neural network implementation and so on at the edge.

References

1. https://www.kdnuggets.com/2017/10/edge-analytics.html
2. https://www.ibm.com/blogs/internet-of-things/edge-iot-analytics/
3. https://www.networkworld.com/article/3224893/what-is-edge-computing-and-how-it-s-changing-the-network.html
4. https://www.ge.com/digital/blog/what-edge-computing
5. IoT Edge Computing, ThoughtWorks, HackerEarth Webinar

Chapter 4
Introduction to Enterprise IoT

Abstract Having understood the significance and working principles of Internet of Things in the previous chapters, this chapter introduces the special variant of Internet of Things which is called as Enterprise IoT or Industrial IoT. The application of Internet of Things in industries is the major focus among all the technology enthusiasts. The industrial IoT is the application of IoT in various industrial domains such as manufacturing, retail, healthcare, energy, supply chain management and logistics etc., It is an extension of robotics and industrial automation with more advanced intelligence and smartness by connecting everything to internet. This chapter tries to address the differences between consumer IoT and Industrial IoT in the beginning and analyses a set of Enterprise IoT applications as a case study to understand the characteristics and potential of Enterprise IoT. The various components of Enterprise IoT are discussed in the next section where everything involved in an Enterprise IoT application from the physical layer level devices to the higher-level applications and solutions. The Enterprise IoT as a technology area, is not evolving very smoothly, but with plenty of challenges. This chapter discusses some of the most important challenges for Enterprise IoT on which several research works are going on in industries and academic institutions. When an Enterprise decides to go for an Enterprise IoT solution, there are several important strategical decisions they must take. The winning strategies for any Enterprise IoT stakeholder are provided in the next section. The last part of the chapter is to introduce the advanced trends in Enterprise IoT such as Blockchain, Artificial Intelligence and Advanced analytics with Big data. Thus, this chapter helps the reader to understand the various aspects of Enterprise Internet of Things after acquiring technical background of Internet of Things from the previous chapters. It is going to be foundation for understanding the Architecture and Design of Enterprise IoT in the next chapters.

Keywords Enterprise IoT · Consumer IoT · Data islands

L. S. Jayashree, G. Selvakumar, *Getting Started with Enterprise Internet of Things: Design Approaches and Software Architecture Models*,
https://doi.org/10.1007/978-3-030-30945-9_4

Learning Objectives

- To understand the differences between consumer Internet of Things and Enterprise Internet of Things
- To learn the different components of enterprise Internet of Things from hardware devices to higher level applications
- To understand the various challenges in the design and implementation of Enterprise IoT
- To study the recommended strategies for successful IoT implementation in Enterprises.

4.1 Introduction

We have a detailed discussion on the fundamentals of Internet of Things in the previous chapters. Initially, The Internet of Things applications were mostly found in consumer-oriented market segments and for individual users. The solutions were related to home automation or connected vehicles or simple household applications. However, in the due course of time, IoT has started revolutionizing industrial sector too. The business implications of Internet of Things are revolutionary and the impact of it in the revenue of the companies is getting more and more significant.

Enterprise IoT refers to the scope of application of Internet of Things in a bigger organizational perspective. Every organization has various kinds of assets and resources which are to be monitored, controlled and assessed for various operational reasons. IoT solutions are adopted in Enterprises more and more to augment the core business activities also it enables establishing new business models and creating more effective customer management. Examples are ranging from a manufacturing industry to fleet operator where the combination of sensor data and sophisticated analytical algorithms has allowed companies to streamline business processes, increase productivity, and develop leading-edge products.

Industrial IoT (IIoT), primarily focuses on utilizing the IoT capabilities in industrial applications. Agriculture, Manufacturing, Healthcare providers, supply chain management & logistics, oil and gas and almost all the industrial sectors have started to explore the applications of Internet of things for various problem areas. IoT promises huge results in terms of revenue, safety, monitoring and management in every business unit of an Enterprise.

The Internet of Things is found to be useful for the three primary reasons in the companies:

Cost reduction – The end to end process management can be administered very well in all the stages. General administration, supply chain management, design and production departments, distribution, sales and all other functional units can be administered effectively

Quality improvement – The cost of quality can be minimized by employing more intelligent predictive maintenance techniques.

Regulatory compliance – Availability of data from every corner makes an information rich environment which reduces the cost of conformance.

The technical aspects for development of customer oriented IoT and Industrial IoT are almost the same. However, there are few significant differences among the above two in terms of requirements gathering, sustainability expectations, revenue generation etc..

4.2 What Is an Enterprise IoT Solution?

An Enterprise IoT solution is a complete IT system which broadly has the following functionalities.

1. Collecting data from various assets like machines, buildings, electrical equipment etc., in an industry with the help of appropriate protocols.
2. Collected data is sent to the backend applications. The backend services of an IoT solution usually enable remote monitoring and control of devices and assets, gather device-related data, and are integrated with other enterprise applications.
3. The background services are implemented to perform any business specific operation like sending alerts, notifications etc., based on the data received from the hardware layer. Also the data is stored in the back end for detailed analytics based on the functional requirements of the business. Also the data will be made available to the users in terms of web and mobile interfaces. The interface would enable the users to monitor the status of assets in real time along with the results of analytical operations.
4. Finally, the collected data is used for operations like preventive maintenance, monitoring and control, prediction and estimation etc., with the help of advanced analytics tools, Artificial Intelligence and Machine learning wherever necessary.

The requirements for enterprises are more complicated when compared to the non-enterprise IoT solutions. Figure 4.1 illustrates the various components located

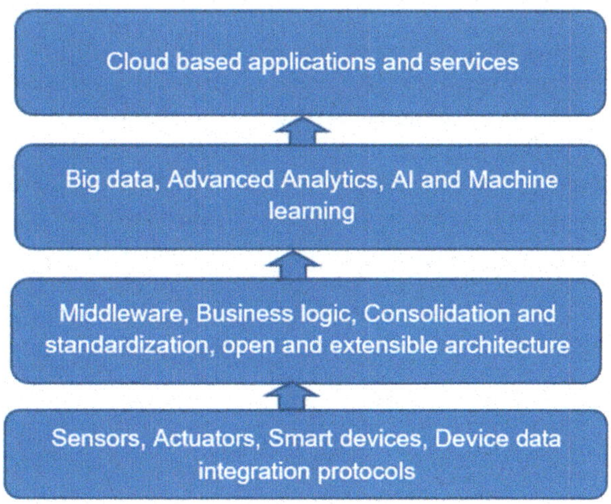

Fig. 4.1 Integrated view of enterprise IoT application

in different layers of an Enterprise IoT solution. The device layer in the bottom comprises of sensors and other devices which are responsible for data collection and transmission. They follow specific protocols to communicate the data collected from the real world to the other components of the system.

The data collected from various devices follow different standards and data types. We have protocols and middleware technologies to consolidate the data and apply the business logic on them. In the top layers we have advanced technologies to handle the collected data and to enable processing by other components of the system.

The communication mechanism between the bottom layers and the application services are significant part of the entire IoT solution. In many cases, the hardware and software components of the solution are deployed on the physical world entity which is called as asset. The on-asset hardware serves as a gateway that enables communication among the other layers. The on-asset software manages the local agent and enables local data integration and related tasks. For instance, a GSM module can be used to communicate remotely with the application or backend services while an industrial bus can be used for integration of collected data.

The Enterprise IoT solutions must be integrated with various applications and components to solve the specific problem. ERP, CRM, PLM are few such applications which directly receive data from IoT solutions. In many cases the Enterprises already have well-built legacy applications which needs to be integrated with the new IoT solution.

Majority of technology officials in enterprises feel that they need to include enterprise IoT initiatives in their future and strategic road maps despite several challenges in implementing it.

Enterprise IoT can help improving several functional units in the organization. Mostly manufacturing and service operations are voted top among all of them. Manufacturing plants experience resource and process optimization as their most significant impact from IoT solutions. Reducing the energy utilization, maximizing asset utilization and ensuring high quality output are very critical objectives which can be met by the IoT integration with manufacturing units.

Service operations have diagnostics, monitoring and predictive maintenance as their significant areas of concern. The Fig. 4.2 depicts many of the areas where IoT can positively impact the Enterprise. Beyond technical implications IoT benefits the Enterprise in strengthening the customer relationships, creating new business models, ensuring quality of services etc., When all the critical assets of an Enterprise are connected and the data is continuously captured, there are no limits to the possibilities of new solutions. Advanced Analytics techniques, Artificial Intelligence and Machine learning, Big data analytics and similar areas continuously contribute to get effective solutions from an Enterprise IoT eco system [2].

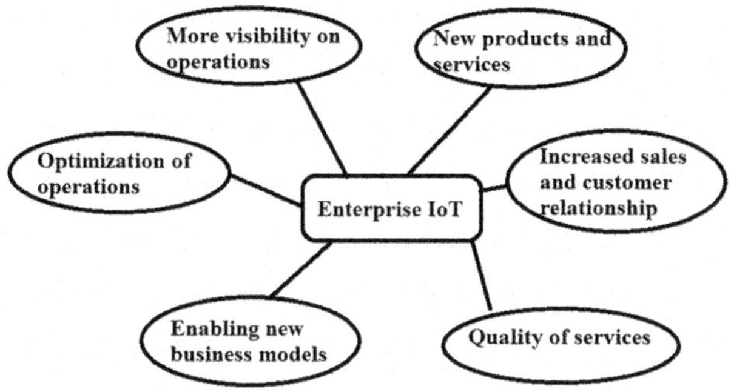

Fig. 4.2 The consequences of enterprise IoT application

4.3 Consumer IoT Vs Enterprise IoT

The functionalities of IoT and IIoT are technically similar. The differences are not very obvious without considering the special requirements in terms of functionalities, architecture, scalability and other factors. Here we use the terms Industrial IoT and Enterprise IoT interchangeably. Though the term Enterprise covers more business-related aspects then the term Industry, In our context we do not have much difference between Industrial IoT and Enterprise IoT. Well, let's look at the differences between Consumer IoT and Industrial IoT solutions. If we look at the hardware layer, both consumer IoT devices and Industrial IoT devices are doing the same task. It may be an activity tracker or health monitoring device deployed in consumer and IIoT space, we can see that in both cases they collect same data which is heart rate information. But there are some quite important factors which differentiates IoT from IIoT which are explained in the following section.

4.3.1 Security Standards

Almost all the IoT devices used today have vulnerabilities and the most important challenge to be faced by the enterprises are the cyber security. Security breaches in the domestic sector such as smart home solutions are implications in the personal privacy. However, in Industrial IoT systems where there are numerous sensors connected to critical resources of the industry the repercussions are extremely high. Take the case of a nuclear power plant or overseas logistics solutions, where the lack of security would cost enormous loss of wealth and it is a danger to national security also. A compromised water management system or some similar smart city solution of a town would stop the daily livelihood of thousands of families and it would cause severe business losses too. A small interruption would cost millions of dollars in a high-volume manufacturing industry if there is a security compromise. If the small electrical grid is hacked, it will directly affect the economic activity for millions of people, companies and it is a great danger to the public security. Thus, Security is critical in Enterprise IoT solutions when compared to the consumer IoT solutions. To face the security related challenges, Enterprise solutions make use of a variety of sophisticated security measures, from resilient system architectures to highly effective business processes. Threat detection, encryption and authentication technologies and other means of security are followed religiously in every part of Enterprise IoT solution.

4.3.2 Robustness and Fault Tolerance

The life span of Industrial IoT systems are usually very large and in some cases it goes beyond decades. The environment in which they get operated are most of the time very harsh. Extreme temperature, pressure, vibration and other polluted conditions are very common. And they may get operated in far flung regions from their office locations. In spite of all these conditions, we expect the enterprise systems should have high availability, less failure rate, more reliability year on year. The shutdown happens only for maintenance. Downtime is not an option for mission critical industrial systems. Resilience or fault tolerance in these systems are prime requirements without which there will be more loss than any good to the company. The operations should be completed at least to a minimum level even though there is loss of connectivity, minor failures etc., This has to be considered from the design phase itself.

The devices used in the industrial IoT systems may need to be submerged in liquids like water or oil. They should meet very strict standards which are not required for consumer IoT devices. Even in few occasions, the components are required to be designed to withstand explosives.

4.3.3 Interoperability

Consumer IoT systems need to have interface with more simple control mechanisms whereas the Enterprise IoT has very complex requirements to interact with other control systems of the industry such as PLC Controllers. Interoperability is a crucial parameter where we have plenty of legacy technologies like SCADA, M2M and other operational technologies. These legacy systems are going to be continued in the near future and the Enterprise IoT solutions should be designed considering the communication with all these systems. There are plenty of protocols and data formats involve in any industrial space where we should ensure that no system is disconnected by the introduction of IoT. Moreover, there are software systems like ERP which has to be integrated without conflicts. Consumer IoT does not have any of these complications.

4.3.4 Scalability

Every Enterprise solution has chance to expand both vertically and horizontally in the long run. The Enterprise systems are usually built as large scale networks which can withstand thousands of controllers, machines and other applications. IoT solutions developed on these environments must expand themselves whenever there is a new addition of sensors or controllers. If we look at the growth of many enterprises, it is beyond imagination when we consider the humble beginning. The solution that we design should incorporate the future expansions of enterprises, whereas this is not at all required for consumer IoT since the life time of these solutions are very little comparatively.

4.3.5 Precision and Accuracy

A millisecond or 0.01 Celsius of temperature may not be significant for a consumer. However, Enterprises require higher levels of precision and accuracy. Automated manufacturing operations need synchronization of several machines which are done with the precision of milliseconds. Quality assurance systems should take remedial actions even if there is extremely small variations in some of the critical parameters. A 1 min of downtime may impact heavily on revenue and safety the Enterprise IoT system should ensure high precision and accuracy throughout the system which is not mandatory in consumer IoT.

4.3.6 Specific to the Industry

Consumer IoT solutions are developed for mass-market. They are not specific to each customer. They are mostly generic solutions to common problems. Basically they are smart products. However, Enterprise solutions are to be developed according to the very specific requirements of the Enterprise. Higher degree of customization is required from the device to software systems. This includes sensors, actuators, controllers, APIs, platforms etc.,

4.3.7 *Communication and Power Requirements*

Remote desert areas, below the surface level of oceans and high-altitude terrains are some of the challenging places where IIoT sensors are installed in several occasions to measure various parameters. Even in the normal factory conditions, it may not be possible all the time to access these sensors due to temperature and other challenging conditions. Human personnel cannot access these assets for maintenance or other requirements. Due to this, IIOT devices should be designed to have maximum possible battery life. The industrial grade batteries are must for IIoT devices. We cannot expect usual cellular networks to support IioT environment due to the above stated reasons, and we need unique, low-power, low bandwidth requirements for communication. Exclusive network families and protocols have been developed for connecting these devices to central servers. These are all not required in the case of consumer IoT and they can survive with the usual WiFi or Bluetooth which are not scalable and limited in their usage. The IIoT systems should be configured with special as well as conventional networking technologies. The IIoT devices are required to be fully remotely controllable which is not required in case of conventional systems.

4.3.8 *Maintenance and Operations*

Maintenance of IIoT systems over its entire life cycle is a critical requirement which is very challenging to meet. The life span of them are also very lengthier when compared to the consumer IoT systems, so planning for maintenance cycle is very critical in IIoT to ensure the higher performance levels. Replacing the sensors and other devices, updating the firmware and other related maintenance activities are crucial requirements of Industrial IoT. Most of the operations in enterprise systems should be highly automated and enabling intelligence in the edge devices are critical. Consumer IoT systems does not have all these complexities. Apart from all these, the industrial and manufacturing environments should provide greater level of flexibility and adaptability to support various operations.

The system designers, engineers and product managers should ensure that the above parameters are considered before they start implementing the solutions. Even though the Industrial and Consumer IoTs does the basic job of connecting physical world and cyber world, they differ significantly in all the above discussed parameters. The Industrial Internet Connectivity Framework (IICF) has been published by The Industrial Internet Consortium, a global non-profit organization. It was founded in 2014 and addressing various problems in IIoT related to standards. The published framework is a blueprint of connectivity standards and a reference architecture for designing interoperable solutions.

4.4 A Peek on Enterprise IoT Applications

In this section we are observing few case studies of Enterprise IoT to understand its functional dimensions in a better way.

Enterprises see the primary benefit of IoT adoption as a positive Return on Investment (ROI) and this can be realized in the form of efficiency gains, cost reductions or even opening new business models that were previously considered infeasible or unattainable. New manufacturing ecosystems that are driven by self-aware, autonomic machines have become realizable with the integration of IoT with the enabling technologies like artificial intelligence, machine learning etc.

In a recent white paper developed by Cisco, the company discusses the various opportunities where the massive amount of data generated by the expanding Internet of Things (IoT). There are four significant process transformation goals addressed in this white paper:

- Enhanced quality of products and services
- Reduced costs with Operational expenditure savings
- Improved decision-making
- Faster innovation

While most companies currently focus on simply connecting machines, devices and other "things," this whitepaper outlines strategies to help industrial operations capture valuable data and insights that can be pulled from newly connected devices. New skill development and Information technology / Operations Technology (IT/OT) collaboration will be paramount when learning how to integrate, automate and analyse this wealth of IoT data and bring industrial operations to the next level [5].

There are plenty of industrial areas where Internet of Things has proved the significance of connected environment and the following sections briefly address few of the areas.

4.4.1 Smart Manufacturing

In manufacturing environments, IIoT enables systems that are driven by self-aware, autonomic machines that could alert engineers about potential mechanical breakdowns of heavy machinery thus, saving huge cost, hours of down time and sometimes even invaluable human lives.

There are environments where production requires the assembly of large, heavy equipment, fabrication of complex electronic components, and precise mechanical alignment like aircraft manufacturing. High levels of quality assurance is ensured by using IIoT.

For example, think about a company which works with its ERP software provider (SAP) to improve efficiency in operations and provide predictive maintenance. The use of real-time analytics from sensors on customers' equipment to develop a predictive analytics capability and enable pre-emptive maintenance will significantly improve the quality standards and reduces the cost of production.

Manufacturing companies use some of the proprietary IoT standards to transport data from the sensors on its equipment and machineries to the cloud. Microsoft Azure, the cloud platform they use, provides the analytics engine. By monitoring their equipment in real time they are able to perform valuable data analysis and implement effective predictive maintenance. This reduces downtime, reduce mean time to repair and improved energy efficiency by fixing poorly operating components. This would benefit a lot to these companies which could never be imagined without the Internet of Things.

Remote monitoring is a critical requirement in manufacturing industry. One of the biggest challenges for manufacturing industry is maintaining the performance of their equipment. The unplanned downtime has to be minimized if the environment is susceptible to extreme weather conditions. Predictive analytics identifies impending equipment problems early and helps avoid unexpected catastrophic failures.

The Industrial Internet is driving new generations of advanced control for manufacturing systems through technologies, connectivity and interoperability. Performance and environmental intelligence can be deployed at any level from the sensor to the cloud to enhance overall system performance.

4.4.2 Smart Health Care

Health care has grown as one of the largest industries of the globe and the challenges to be solved also has increased. Smart health care tries to address many of the challenges with Internet of Things. The smart health care goes beyond providing remote assistance to the patient. The full potential of smart health care can be realized in the Enterprise level solutions where the Internet of Things has been observed to produce the following outcomes.

- Efficient and transparent management of drugs
- Eliminating system errors
- Assessment and improvement of treatment outcomes
- Management of diseases related data
- Improving patient experience
- Minimizing the operational cost
- Emergency healthcare

4.4.3 Supply Chain Management and Logistics

The Internet of Things revolution has affected nearly every global industry from retail to connected vehicles. One of the most exciting areas of impact is the global supply chain. The IoT is set to revolutionize the supply chain with both operational efficiencies and revenue opportunities. In today's market, supply chain isn't just a way to keep track of products. It's a way to gain an edge on competitors and completely remodel the way businesses operate.

The operational efficiency of an Enterprise hugely depends upon the relationship among various trading partners such as suppliers, vendors or customers. The IoT improves the quality of communication among the various stack holders which ultimately enhances the quality of business and the relationships. Manufacturing industry makes use of Internet of Things tremendously in their supply chains to track their assets. The tracking numbers and bar codes are not solving all the challenges in tracking and monitoring the assets. The RFID and GPS sensors can track the products from the manufacturing floor to the retail store. At any point in time, supply chain managers can use these sensors to obtain data like the temperature at which an item was stored, how long it spent in cargo, and even how long it took to fly off the shelf. The type of data gained from the IoT can help companies get a tighter grip on quality control, on-time deliveries, and product forecasting.

The inventory control systems have become extremely powerful with the help of IoT. The sensors can provide far more accurate inventories than humans can do. Amazon has started using WiFi robots to scan QR codes on various products and to track them. If the manufacturing company could track the inventory including the supplies for future manufacturing very conveniently on their mobile screens, no longer the case of missing deadlines. All the data gained through the IoT can be even used to analyze the trends and optimize the schedules in manufacturing and logistics.

4.4.4 Energy

In industries like energy generation, IoT has already started producing substantial impact. In sectors renewable energy front, monitoring and management of solar panels, inverters, distribution and load balancing components and other critical parts is essential in order to maximize uptime and to ensure performance.

Fluctuation in power requirements, health and efficiency of devices, connectivity, and other issues can be solved by implementing IoT in solar power stations. The same reasons are quite valid in Windmills also. While the world is moving towards unconventional energy sources, the major problem has been the cost of energy. New operation models with the help of Internet of Things would definitely play a major role making unconventional and clean energy production feasible in the near future.

The success of enterprise IoT will be driven by technical innovations and services that enable it. Tools like a scalable and secure IoT platform that operates in real-time, low power/low-cost hardware to power devices and modern networks to transmit data are the building blocks for enterprise IoT, as well as consumer IoT to change how we operate and live.

In the big picture, the technology is ready and the need is there to drive IoT forward. While consumer services will certainly improve quality of life, enterprise IoT will face down some of the biggest challenges facing the world today:

4.5 The Components of Enterprise IoT

The Enterprise IoT stack is a combination of different layers. Each layer has a group of hardware and/or software components that communicate with the other layers. Primarily there are devices or communication and sensing hardware in the base layer which sense the physical parameters and send the data to the subsequent layers through different protocols. The higher-level platforms are responsible for management of underlying devices and data produced from them. There is a middleware layer to accommodate different types of proprietary devices, components, software etc., While the data is finally obtained, Enterprise IoT makes use of Analytics platforms to analyze the data which is getting streamed continuously or the data which has been stored already. Next, there is a cognitive layer to get the insights from the collected data. On top of all of these there is a solutions layer where the end user consumes the solutions [1]. We would illustrate the above concepts in detail in this section. Apart from these functional components, there are non-functional requirements including security, device management, application security, user management, service management etc., (Fig. 4.3)

4.5.1 Solutions and Applications

When an enterprise wants to have an IoT based solutions, the initial requirement is the vision they have in transforming their existing business model by incorporating IoT. Every application in the real world can be imagined as a set of some data management or data processing activities. Clearly defining the applications in the initial

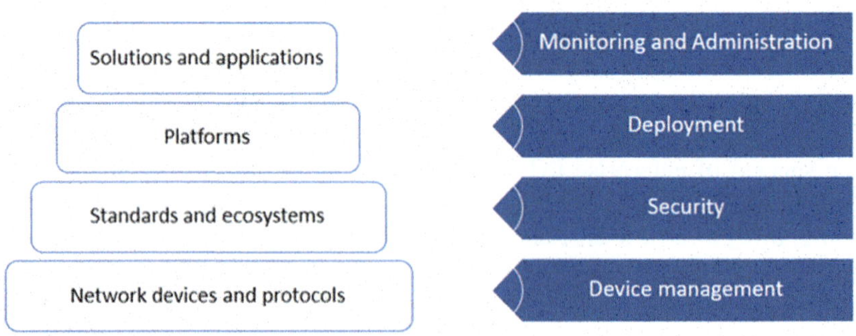

Fig. 4.3 The components of an enterprise IoT application

stage helps in drilling down to appropriate platforms, tools, hardware devices and protocols.

Solution models are collection of services and standards developed for one common problem area. For example, connected healthcare is a solution which has clearly defined tasks and services. It is like an abstract model which illustrates the functionalities in a broader level. Applications are extended from the solution models for a very specific industry. The solution model is 'connected healthcare' and the application can be 'Intelligent health care system for hospital ABC'. The application makes use of the framework provided by the solution model and customizes the components in a more detailed manner.

Solution is the term used to refer the complete set of applications, components and processes developed to solve a problem. The strategic planners, technical designers and human resource officials design the high level solution for the Enterprises and during Enterprise IoT solution develop they consider everything from the return on investment to available human skills and sustainability of the solution in future. They start with building an abstract data model of the problem domain. Abstract data model is nothing but collection of information that represents the state and behavior of an object. For a connected vehicle system, the details about the car, driver, engine, the current location, speed, charges applicable for the vehicle, revenue generated by the car in the last few months, tax implications and similar data. This model is used for defining the use cases of the solution. The use cases are part of the application to be developed. Here they come up with the primary objectives of the solution such as, remotemonitoring, predictive maintenance or geospatial analysis.

4.5.2 Platforms

In the huge IoT environment there are several hardware and software components, different standards and protocols. IoT platform is the component that supports or enables communication among all the components. The IoT Platform ensures that the hardware layer level devices and the network components are properly utilized and the higher level application requirements are met. Or we can even say that, the IoT platform helps to design the higher level enterprise solutions accoriding to the capabilities of underlying devices.

The primary services provided by IoT platforms are given below.

- Device configuration, device management and device monitoring. The security and firmware updates also has to be taken care of.
- Data collection, communication and management
- Higher level application development, analytics and visualization.
- Connectivity to the other systems of the Enterprise like ERP, Human Resource, Finance etc.,

- User management. Management of people's credentials, permissions and custom report generation etc.,
- There are several proprietary and open source IoT platforms are available in the market. Chapter 6 discusses IoT platforms in detail.

4.5.3 Standards and Eco Systems

The technology stack of an Enterprise IoT system can be viewed as multiple layers of components. In each layer a specific kind of hardware and software components are used. They function according to the protocols and standards followed by their manufacturers. The combination of multiple components across layers create the IoT ecosystem. Wifi, Bluetooth, LPWAN are the protocols are used in the transportation layer level. For device identification and infrastructure there are plenty of standards such as EPC, uCode, 6LowPAN, RPL etc., In data management we have MQTT, CoAP, AMQP, Websocket etc., JSON-LD, Web thing model are the higher level semantic standards available. It is kind of a difficult task to design an end to end solution by composing all these diverse elements which is usually taken care by the IoT platforms. Apart from these, there are other security and quality oriented standards and protocols also play a role in an enterprise IoT system.

4.5.4 Network, Devices and Protocols

The term 'Things' in IoT refers to the hardware devices around us which are not usually connected to Internet like a computer or a mobile phone. IoT makes it possible that every device in our environment can be connected to the internet, thus transforming our physical world parameters into digital information which is available in the internet. Anything available in the internet increases the scope to perform analytics, decision making, control and monitoring and other activities. The hardware devices segment is highly fragmented with plenty of device manufacturers who have embraced the IoT at present. The number of companies is keep on increasing. Initially we had embedded devices which have an electronic component called microcontroller that has the capability to give a digital face to any machine like washing machine or air conditioning unit. Sometimes they have a small operating systems to drive the units to provide an user interface and to make control and monitoring operations. This is the basis of IoT, in which we provide more networking capabilities and expand the range of devices from washing machines and air conditioning units to everything possible. Fitness bands, Heart rate monitors, vehicles, parts of vehicles like tires, thermostate, web camera, door lock, even a chair or a shoe can become a part of IoT, a 'Thing'.

4.5.5 *Other Concerns*

4.5.5.1 IoT Security and Management

Connecting everything to internet obviously increases the security risks. Especially in enterprises security of data is a very sensitive issue. When multiple players like hardware manufacturers, network administrators, platform providers, application developers, system integrators the complexity of integration of the solution becomes enormous and maintaining the security standard is very challenging. Enterprise IoT stack usually expected to come with a set of tools to manage the security and performance issues.

4.5.5.2 Device Management

Hardware engineers or embedded system specialists take care of device management in which they take care of device registration, device communication to middleware, device troubleshooting and firmware updates as and when it is required. Every device has its own replica in the digital space which is called as digital twins popularly. This makes it possible to monitor and control the devices anywhere from the world. Device management includes management of gateways and local storage. Edge computing advancements are making the device management more interesting as well as complicated. The enterprise IoT platform provides administration console to manage the devices securely. It also takes care of APIs to register and monitor the devices. The kind of operations the devices permitted to do as per the application requirements will be controlled by the platforms. Because not all the device would require the ability to communicate to cloud, since it may require only one way communication capability to cloud to get firmware updates. These restrictions can be controlled through the interfaces.

4.5.5.3 Monitoring and Administration

The life cycle of the devices is another important to be controlled by the IoT system. The registration, begin, suspend and stop activities of the devices or the ability to invoke specific commands or event handling activities has to be monitored by the system. Depends upon the use cases the states of the system will vary so that the administration requirements. Software installation, libraries used, connection status/data communication on a specific day and all similar parameters has to be monitored and administered. There might a storage space problem which prevents a gateway to function properly. This may be due to a malfunction of a synchronization service which failed to clear the data as per the scheduler. The monitoring system should address these and take remedial actions at the earliest possible time. Also the suspicious actions and similar unexpected behaviors of the system also has to be monitored carefully. Administrative commands take care of auto update of libraries and other software components. Device manufacturers, middleware developers and cloud service providers are partnering with each other to make the remote administration more easier.

4.5.5.4 Deployment

When it comes to deployment the IoT system has to be seen in a holistic manner from the device layer to application layer by taking care of all non functional requirements like security. There are several innovations happening in the deployments in terms virtualization. Docker images are recently used for light weight deployments and containerization. Similar to DoS (Denial of Service) attacks, there are Denial of Sleep attacks which uses malicious code which is spread across the Internet with the objective of draining the batteries of devices by preventing them to go to sleep state when not in use. The deployment mechanism needs to take care of several performance attributes and security issues. Impersonating 'things', encrypting communications and other similar practices are followed to increase the security. Sophisticated backend is another.

4.6 Challenges in Enterprise IoT

The global market for IoT enabled solutions are on the rise as per several surveys and research reports conducted by magazines and other technical societies. The projections are clearly indicating that numerous Enterprises have started exploring IoT in their business areas. Behind all the expectations and hype there are a plenty of challenges for IoT adoption in enterprises. The enterprises are facing significant barriers in their IoT initiatives despite of the anticipated benefits and support from all the stakeholders of the business. Not only the establishment of IoT ecosystem, but also maintenance of the IoT applications is also giving lots of apprehensions to the technical managers. Because they must function reliably and predictably to avoid huge complications and losses in the business process. Unlike other systems, cyber physical systems are complicated to maintain and to debug in case of problems. So it comes with the requirements for periodical maintenance and special care. In this section, we are going to see some of the important challenges which are seen as road blocks for IoT adoption in enterprises.

4.6.1 Determining the Real Business Value of IoT in Enterprise Landscape

As an emerging technology IoT gives huge promises to Enterprises about innovative business process management possibilities and accelerated growth in terms of revenue and productivity. However, Enterprises in various sectors such as mechanical or civil the Enterprises should find out the actual value of incorporating IoT in their businesses. It should not become a bottleneck in the long run. Deciding if IoT is suitable for a particular use case has to be analyzed well before investing money and other resources. Several Enterprises have experienced loss of money and time by adopting new technologies by their fancy promises without making proper analysis. So, the first challenge is to find out potential use cases in which IoT can be introduced which could benefit the organization as well as the customers in a more sustainable manner. Getting the data from physical world or the assets of an organization is meaningful only when the insights obtained from them prove to be beneficial without doubt. Enterprises solve this problem by several brain storming sessions with the stake holders who different backgrounds and deeply analyzing the case studies and samples from other companies. The success of implementing IoT in an Enterprise starts from errorless problem identification and problem description with proper outcome expectations. The efficiency, improved productivity and customer satisfaction are some of the major outcomes which has to be mapped with the IoT incorporation in an Enterprise which is a task that needs quite some effort by the management. So they have to work on figuring out key performance indicators to measure which are expected to be improved by introducing IoT. The executives when drafting for IoT strategy they have tough time in estimating the impact in operating costs and other expenses by introducing IoT. Mostly the approval is done by the board members of the Enterprise who are not keen on the innovative potential of the technology in future but the business value in immediate to short term.

4.6.2 Security Concerns

When we look at an end to end IoT solution, security threats are present from the beginning to end. From the hardware devices and network to the higher level applications where the data is stored and processed, security needs to be ensured. Because the security processes in individual components of an IoT chain are not uniform and the weakest link of the chain becomes the cause of vulnerability of the whole system.

Recognizing and authenticating the endpoint devices that are present in the company's network continuously is not an easier job. The flow of data has to be secured from all the devices which are connected to the system. Moreover, Enterprises should have adequate processes to handle if there is a threat or breach of standards. A single standard or practise cannot solve the problems in an IoT ecosystem due to the presence of various components with different nature. To address this, the organization needs a holistic cybersecurity framework. The devices have to be managed carefully with appropriate authentication and they have to be terminated if there is an issue. The IoT sensors are usually installed throughout the enterprise environment and making them more secure by following standards and processes increases the annual IT security budget remarkably. The vulnerability increases hugely because of newly added potential entry points for security breaches. It increases the risk of business several times. IoT malware attacks are in the rising and the security community is still addressing the common patterns of these attacks to design the protection mechanisms. Protecting the intellectual property of the enterprise is always of highest importance. The increased incidents of ransomeware attacks are not a good news for enterprises who want to adopt IoT in their systems. The entire industrial network is exposed to internet is a situation where we need more than one solution and security policies with very careful attention to details. This is one of the more significant factor which makes Enterprises to think about IoT. The threats are unprecedented similar to the possibilities and the enterprises may follow the basic guidelines mentioned below.

- An IT Security team has to be built with latest tools and skillsets and with greater command over the security policies.
- Along with other factors, security risk has to play a role in identifying the priority of an asset. A web camera may be a minor asset with less impact on productivity, but in terms of security risk it has to be prioritized appropriately dpends on the business scenario.
- Anything that comes from the cloud such as software or firmware updates should be activated only after a careful inspection.
- The new device management has to be done with utmost caution to prevent the intrusion of malicious devices.
- Distributed denial of service attacks should be given more importance and continuous monitoring of all connected devices should be done to monitor the traffic.
- All the stakeholders and partner organizations also should be made to function with same guidelines in mind.

4.6.3 Compatibility with Legacy Systems

When the Enterprise is a long standing one, it must be having lot of disparate systems who never needed communication with each other. These legacy systems were not designed for any communication possibilities. Generating or consuming digital date from those legacy systems may be impossible. It may not be efficient to digitalize other modern systems alone because the entire system would require all the components should work with similar capabilities. Data collection from only a part of the entire system may not bring any effective solution. Modernizing all the legacy systems is absolutely beyond the financial gains expected from introducing IoT in several cases. It is considered to be one of the biggest challenges of IoT implementation. For example, in a health care organization it may be possible to connect all the devices from thermometer, pacemakers to advanced scanning machines. But if the data processing software has no possibility of connecting with internet or any other communication related limitation, the entire healthcare system can never experience IoT based solutions. The solution in most of the cases is, the hardware vendors are trying hard to manufacture new components which can work with legacy system to bridge the gap.

4.6.4 IoT Integration

In the last section, we discussed integration problems with the legacy systems. At the same time, integration with other modern system of the Enterprise also create difficulties in many occasions. The efforts made to manage the integration has affected the information and operation productivity in several situations.

To handle this challenge, Enterprises draft long term plans in adopting to new standards which would be compatible with one another in the due course. Most of the integration problems are solved by properly using IoT middleware. However, choosing the middleware which is appropriate for all the business units of the Enterprise is a tough one. The platform must satisfy other non-functional requirements of the Enterprise also. Chapter 6 discusses in detail about the requirements of IoT platforms and the things to be considered while choosing the IoT platforms. The operations technology (OT) and the information technology (IT) of an Enteprise work in a very different style and using different solution architectures. Integration among them has to be done very carefully without creating problems for data security.

4.6.5 Data Management

When hundreds of or thousands of devices are collecting data non-stop, whet we get is a huge amount of data to store and analyse. In huge enterprises where the number of devices go beyond millions there may not be facilities to handle this amount of data. Handling all the data generated by all IoT end point devices creates serious questions like "How to manage this data? And what kind of information technology background the enterprise has to handle this data?"

Another important question is how to convince all the stakeholders that the data generated can be used for some effective analysis and it can yield some valuable outcome to the Enterprise.

Many IoT platforms provide the facilities to collect and analyse the data, but it is the right frame of mind that decides how to use those in such a way that it actually benefits the organization. The problem is about creating the dashboards to look at the data, but the significance of the insights in driving the business. Another perspective of this challenge is nature of data. The data is becoming more unstructured nowadays due to diversity in the sources. Analysing the data demands more specific skill sets and capabilities in the organization. Before that, determining which is the quality data among the available data is a very important concern, because all the data collected is not actionable data. The enterprises need NoSQL format data storage mechanisms to store all these unstructured data. There bigdata frameworks such as Hadoop and Cassandra are reducing the complexity in this regard to a great extent. The Enterprises should be ready to make use of these advancements before entering into IoT adoption.

When the Enterprises adopt IoT solutions without a proper data strategy data islands are created. Data islands are data which are created without relationship to the context of enterprise data strategy created and followed by the CXOs. Without proper data governance, the date gets siloed and this islanded data creates organizational challenges.

Manually integrating it and bringing it in the radars of enterprise data strategy is time consuming and resource intensive. The value of the data would be lost by the time the data is organized and integrated.

4.6.6 Project Duration

When we introduce IoT in fully functional Enterprise systems, it may take a more time than expected to evaluate the outcomes. Because enterprises usually suffer from the resistance of employees when a change is introduced. Moreover, when IoT is introduced, there may changes in the existing business models which prolong the project duration. It also impacts the cultural arrangement of the company. All these factors together, the time estimations for introducing IoT in new projects is usually uncertain and Enterprises think about it more seriously.

4.6.7 Standardization

When bigger companies like Apple and Google start developing IoT solutions, they prefer not to allow any possibilities of communication with outside technical world. They want to control the ecosystems by their own products and standards. If a company provides electricity related or an emergency fire alarm management solution for an Enterprise, this may not go well with the company's central heating system. The products developed by companies are not easily interoperable or at least communicating with each other. When there is an interoperability or lack of standardization issue, there are questions about sustainability in the long term. Without long term assurance of these solutions, Enterprises may not adopt them comfortably. Even though larger organizations are generally reluctant to make their innovations open standards, few companies are trying to build an interoperable IoT system. Axon platform solution is one such interoperable IoT solution. There are few more available in the market. However, they do not completely solve the interoperability problem and still several research works are going on in this direction.

4.7 The Winning Strategies of Enterprise IoT

The fundamentals of Enterprise IoT and the challenges of adopting IoT in Enterprises have been discussed in the previous sections. To overcome those challenges and to get the maximum benefits of IoT the Enterprises should carefully plan their strategies. This section addresses some of the winning strategies to be followed by the Enterprises.

4.7.1 Filling the Capability Gaps

Most of the enterprises work backwards from connected product to the value proposition. In this journey they fail to understand the dimensions of their project completely. One big strategy they have to think about is their plans to fill the capability gaps in the due course of solution development. Most of the projects fail in between due to changing the people frequently due to lack of performance and unable to employ quality people to complete the work within the time limit. Even identifying the skill requirements in the beginning of the project is challenging in many projects due to the changing nature of business and the complicated talent pool requirements at every stage of the development process [4, 5].

It is always advised to form a proper ecosystem which comprises specialists from all the areas such as technology practitioners, domain specialists, sales and marketing people etc., Especially it is most important in large scale projects. The complexities of managing the IoT system development is usually underestimated which becomes the route cause of the failure. To prevent this, we require partnership with qualified people.

Estimation of skill sets and the potential experts we need to build the system has to be done well ahead of the project commencement. A list of very important skills required to complete a typical enterprise IoT project is given below. An IoT enabled manufacturing unit has been taken for consideration. The kind of skills and exper-

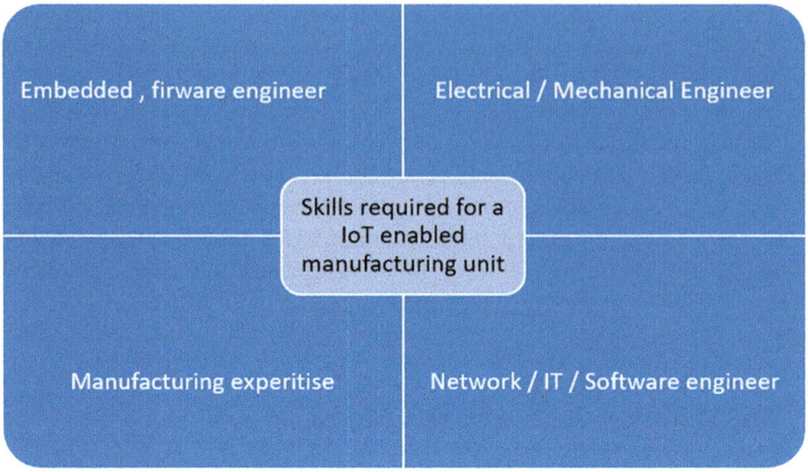

Fig. 4.4 Enterprise IoT – Skill sets

tise may vary drastically depends upon the domain in which we try to build the solution (Fig. 4.4).

4.7.1.1 Embedded, Firmware and Electronics Engineers

Embedded devices are the reprogrammable hardware which forms the basis of infrastructure of the IoT solution. We need specialists to maintain the embedded hardware by installing required firmware and performing troubleshooting activities. Firmware is the operating system of the embedded device which controls the device. A stable firmware architecture is extremely important in the life cycle of an IoT system development. The circuit design and layout of devices in the enterprise is the responsibility of electronics engineers where, they take care of power supply, interface with other components, quality assurance and other similar activities.

4.7.1.2 Electrical and Mechanical Engineers

In a manufacturing unit, multiple machineries are deployed to take care of the production process. Mechanical engineers are responsible for the physical functioning of the equipment and how it interfaces with other systems. They are responsible for the making provisions intended for data collection through incorporating electrical and electronic components. Almost every equipment requires electrical power supply and electrical engineers are taking care of designing and developing the power circuits for the plant and equipment. The point to be noted here is the mechanical and electrical engineers should perform their jobs by keeping the special requirements of enterprise IoT requirements in mind. The mechanical engineers should have the manufacturing expertise also to take care of the production process with proper industrial engineering practices.

4.7.1.3 Networking, IT and Software Engineers

When the IoT system is developed with hardware devices and network connectivity on the core manufacturing units. Now the embedded systems will start collecting the data and send them to the cloud through the networking. The microcontrollers used nowadays have inbuilt network data transmission capabilities with the help of wifi modules. Networking engineers are responsible to ensure that the data is collected from the manufacturing units with adequate quality and transmitted to the destined local repository or cloud. He needs to ensure that the errors, transmission failures and other problems would not occur. Once the data is collected and stored, the application layer activities start. Here the software engineers design and develop software components which are required for analytics and getting insights from the data. In most of the cases a pre-built IoT platform will be used to take care of this process. Software engineers are responsible for working on this platform to ensure that the application is running successfully, proper reports are generated, data is backed up and the requirements of all the end users are satisfied [3].

4.7.2 Balancing Technology and Business

The business and technology are two sides of a same coin. Business drives technology to achieve more and technology supports business to earn more. When the enterprises adopt IoT the important strategy the need to develop is the proportion of business and technology in their solutions. If a perfect balance is not maintained between technology and business the solution may be too technical and not useful or too business oriented and not sustainable in the long run. When IoT brings out the potential of even the smallest devices can generate data and it can participate in creating valuable insights, it tends to transform the business. When the competitors start using the advanced technologies, the Enterprises will think about commencing their own IoT solution development with the fear of being left behind by others. However, identifying appropriate business use cases is extremely important rather than attempting new technologies. There must be adequate Research to be done to spot the opportunities for efficiency, scope of productivity improvement or value addition. This can be done only by identifying meaningful data generated in the ecosystem and the kind of insights it can provide [6].

4.7.3 Managing the Data

Data management is considered as a double-edged sword in Enterprise IoT. Organisations need to plan very carefully about data management principles to satisfy their customers' requirements with adequate security. A solid data security framework maintenance is a continuous process which needs frequent action and review. Data policies, privacy and permission policies, protection policies are the fundamental set of rules which needs to be drafted and communicated to all the stakeholders and enough measures must be taken to adhere to the policies. Basically, the data management policies address the following questions. How the data has to be collected? how it has to be stored? who are the users with access permission to the data? what kind of access permissions are available? Are the access permissions controlled by roles which are predefined? Or Are they any programmatic dynamic decision making to decide data access permissions? Who controls the mission critical data? And many more. Answering these questions has become integral part of IoT strategy since the speed and scale of data received by IoT end points have become extremely huge. Moreover, the data has to be processed in real time with very lesser turnaround time for decision making. These constraints have to be met without violating privacy and other data security related issues. Before the Enterprises start to manage their IoT data they should look at the existing data of their organization and review the security policies. Collecting more IoT over and above the existing data would hurt if there are no proper understanding about the existing and new data. The data strategy is usually collaboratively developed among all the stakeholders including the IT department, business managers, operations managers, plant supervisors and the data security team together [4].

4.7.4 Proof of Concept and Prototyping

Before full deployment of an Enterprise IoT solution, the technical team should experiment the end to end solution with a minimum functional proof of concept. A protoryppe simulates the core functionalities and components of the final solution which is being developed. It is extremely important to answer the following questions, so that the design created by the development team can be validated [7].

- To validate the use cases by obtaining the expected data and making some trial analytics.
- To understand if all the features and data identified in the design phase are sufficient for the complete solution or any discrepancies in the design.
- To identify the challenges which can stop the progress of development when the data becomes huge or the number of users becomes more or any other unforeseen situation.
- To find out the ineffective or useless modules developed during design phase.
- To identify the unaddressed parts of the use cases if any.

There is no fixed methodology to create a prototype. It depends upon the resources and time allocated for the process by the enterprise. Development of an IoT solution is a time consuming and costly process. After investing efforts and money, if the solution does not yield desired outcomes after testing at the end it will be a huge loss for the enterprise. So development of a prototype with minimum core functionalities and to evaluate the design of the solution well ahead of complete implementation is a definite winning strategy.

4.7.5 Integrating IoT with Existing Business Flow

The most important winning strategy in IoT development in an Enterprise is how to integrate it with the existing business operations. Based on the age of the enterprise the process model could be complicated to any extent. When a new workflow is developed with the help of IoT there shouldn't be two different business flows. For example, in a manufacturing unit the health of machineries can be inspected by sensors and the data can be stored in a server. But before the implementation of IoT, the data was collected manually and submitted to the final approval to the plant in charge. Consider the plant in charge person has no access to computers due to his continuous movement and he has smooth access only to smartphones. But if the developed IoT solution has only web-based dash boards and there is no mobile based interface, the plan in charge will follow previous method only. The implemented solution may serve other purposes, but in the predictive maintenance process will happen in the same old fashion. This happens due to the gap in the existing business flow and the change introduced through IoT.

4.8 Conclusion

The technical society has been witnessing the surge of developments in the area of Internet of Things to create the smart world around us. While majority of the attention is in the consumer segment, in the long run, IoT is going to be used primarily in enterprises due to the kind of impact it will create in a large user group as well as its potential to revive the revenue generation of the enterprise. This chapter introduces the Enterprise IoT with all its features and requirements and it elaborately discusses how does it differ from the consumer IoT. When an Enterprise wishes to implement IoT it should have a clear understanding of the challenges ahead and the strategy they have to develop to overcome the challenges. The major portion of this chapter is dedicated to discussing the challenges and winning strategies of Enterprise IoT. This chapter will be a foundation to read through the next chapters where the design and implementation of Enterprise IoT is handled.

References

1. Del Giudice M (2016) Discovering the internet of things (IoT): technology and business process management, inside and outside the innovative firms. Bus Process Manag J 22(2). https://doi.org/10.1108/BPMJ-02-2016-0029
2. Ibarra-Esquer JE, González-Navarro FF, Flores-Rios BL, Burtseva L, Astorga-Vargas MA (2017) Tracking the evolution of the internet of things concept across different application domains. Sensors (Basel) 17(6):1379. Published 2017 Jun 14. https://doi.org/10.3390/s17061379
3. Slama D, Puhlmann F, Mirrish J, Bhatnagar RM (2015) Enterprise IoT, 1st edn. O'Reilly, USA
4. Sinclair B (2017) IoT Inc: how your company can Use the Internet of Things to win in the outcome economy, 1st edn. McGraw-Hill Education, New York
5. Noronha A, Moriarty R, O'Connell K, Villa N, Attaining IoT value: how to move from connecting things to capturing insights gain an edge by taking analytics to the edge, Cisco white paper. https://www.mckinsey.com/featured-insights/internet-of-things
6. https://www.saviantconsulting.com/blog
7. https://www.techuk.org

Chapter 5
Architecture for an Enterprise IoT

Abstract The previous chapter introduces the concept of Enterprise Internet of things with the help of sample applications. This chapter introduces the architectural concerns of Enterprise Internet of Things. The chapter starts with a reference architecture of Enterprise Internet of Things where all the components of an end to end IoT solution is explained. The critical component in the architecture is the middleware solution. The middleware component enables communication across the disparate hardware and software components in the solution. Enterprise IoT solutions are more complicated to develop and maintain due to the participation of several vendors. The interoperability challenges are handled with the help of middleware solutions and this chapter addresses two important architectures namely Monolithic architecture and Microservices architecture. These architectures are not specific to IoT solutions but generic for Enterprise software development. This chapter illustrates how the Microservices architecture is the most suitable choice for designing Enterprise IoT applications. In the last part, there is a detailed discussion on the trade-off between Monolithic and Micro services architectures.

Keywords IoT architecture · Monolithic architecture · Microservices · IoT middleware

Learning Objectives

1. To study the IoT reference architecture to get a comprehensive understanding about the various components involved.
2. To learn the middleware solutions used for Enterprise IoT and their significance.
3. To know the basics of monolithic and microservices architectural patterns and their differences.
4. To study how Microservices can be used in Enterprise IoT Architecture.

L. S. Jayashree, G. Selvakumar, *Getting Started with Enterprise Internet of Things: Design Approaches and Software Architecture Models*,
https://doi.org/10.1007/978-3-030-30945-9_5

5.1 Introduction

The Internet of Things (IoT) creates a disruptive transformation across several areas. Since being invented, the IoT applications have been significantly found in consumer oriented market segments like healthcare and home automation. In parallel bigger companies of the world started exploring the applications of Internet of Things in other areas like agriculture, governance of cities, manufacturing, health care etc.

Industrial IoT (IIoT), specifically focuses on the requirements of industrial applications, such as manufacturing, supply chain management, industrial engineering, oil and gas and utilities. In a larger picture, we may not be able to find much difference in the implementation of Industrial IoT solutions from customer oriented solutions, since the technical components (both hardware and software) involved in the end to end solutions are almost the same (with respect to the sensors, cloud platforms, connectivity and analytics). However, there are several very important aspects that distinguish Enterprise IoT from the other application areas. In this chapter, we try to address those differences which are usually seen from the perspectives of business owners, vendors, delivery managers, customers and other stakeholders of Enterprise IoT Applications.

5.2 IoT Architecture for an Enterprise

Internet of Things cannot be defined in a single Architectural model due to the participation of various hardware, software and protocols or standards. A modular and scalable architecture with a variety of capabilities will be required to understand the complete functionalities of Internet of Things. In Enterprise Internet of Things it gets more complicated due to the expectations from various types of end users and huge amount of data with different formats. Moreover, we need to cover multiple components like server side entities, cloud, networking model that communicate with the devices, agents, edge, middleware etc., However, we are trying to provide a reference architecture which can be a seen as a combination of various entities that enable an Internet of Things application in an Enterprise.

This architecture is for generic reference and it does not specify or emphasize any technology family. The architecture can be extended based on the future advancements in the technology and industrial requirements.

Basically, the reference architecture splits the various components involved into multiple layers [1]. Each layer is dedicated for a specific set of functionalities performed by hardware and software entities. Each layer communicates with the bottom and upper layers using specific communication methodologies and protocols. Collectively the architecture ensures that functional and non-functional requirements of an Enterprise IoT system are satisfied by developing a solution based on the architecture. There are also some entities or functionalities which span across the layers. We present this architecture as simple as possible to enable the readers to understand the basics.

Based on the reference architecture, the various components of an Enterprise IoT system can be divided into following layers.

1. User interface and External communication layer
2. Application management layer with event processing, storage and higher order analytics
3. Enterprise service bus or middleware layer
4. Communication and networking layer
5. Device layer

Access management, Security and User management are the cross-cutting layer activities performed across the layers.

To understand the Enterprise IoT Architecture, we need to approach it with a Reference Architecture in which the roles of each component is illustrated clearly. As the IoT technology has become a recognized way of monitoring the events, several industrial environments and enterprises started implementing it. The data produced by sensors and objects are becoming huge in larger environments and the task is massive to handle the data from all the sensors according to the already complicated business processes. In Enterprises IoT services should coordinate technology, human and business process to quickly interact with the real world across the business domains [2]. Due to the presence of variety of business processes, personal and physical entities, and the changes in physical world the Enterprise IoT is several times complicated to implement.

With the development of technology and necessity to make it useful in enterprises, the IoT application developers have started to consider how to integrate the existing network facilities and the new opportunities in system design. The huge information collected as an outcome of connected environment is further processed and delivered to different applications according to the requirements, then is used to trigger the corresponding collaborative business system. Thus, it would not going to be a single independent technology challenge, but a challenge to be handled in technology, business and management layers of the Enterprise.

Comparatively Enterprise IoT brings new technical challenges to IoT services such as, heterogeneity of hardware, network and operating system, interoperability between applications and services, fusion of massive heterogeneous data, scalability and continuous integration. Available IoT devices (sensors and actuators) are vendors specific where the communication protocols and data exchange formats vary from device to device. The complexity increases exponentially when simple devices are integrated to form a complex network and it is difficult to provide a unified solution for IoT application. In the IoT application environment, several human and non human objects are participating which are following specific data standards and communication platforms. Different platforms lead to great inconvenience for achieving interoperability and mutual communication in IoT applications. Most of the challenges concerned with communication among different layers of Internet of Things is usually handled by Middleware layers. Middleware layers provide necessary abstraction to the device layers and it enables deployment of various methodologies in the higher layers to overcome the above challenges stated.

Device Layer

Any device can be a part of Internet of things if it is provided with a communication mechanism so that it can exchange data with the internet. If they do not have the communication ability naturally, they have to be used with micro controller devices which has direct connectivity to the internet with the help of Wi-Fi or Bluetooth modules attached with them. Some of the devices with direct connections are

- Arduino with Ethernet, Wifi, or GSM
- Raspberry pi with Ethernet, Wifi or GSM
- Intel Galileo

Also, several devices following standards like ZigBee, low power radio devices etc., also can be connected to the internet and they can become a part of the IoT solution.

Each device has to be given with an identity, so that it can be used as an address for communication. The identity can be a chip level unique identifier or provided by the communication sub system such as Bluetooth label or MAC address in Wi-Fi. In some cases the identify is available in the EEPROM itself. The reference architecture recommends that an immutable, permanent UUID has to be provided to each device.

Communication and Networking Layer

The communication layer is responsible for connecting all the devices with each other and to the primary network backbone and to the internet. In this process, we have several communication protocols and the following are few of them.

- HTTP/HTTPS

A simple stateless text-based protocol which is used as a request reply protocol in the application layer and the small devices like 8 bit controllers hardly support it fully. POST and GET are the primary methods of this protocol and to utilize all the capabilities of it the devices need to be 32 bit based.

- MQTT 3.1/3.1.1

MQTT is the protocol optimized for Internet of Things. It was invented to support embedded system and SCADA. This protocol is a publish-subscribe messaging system based on a broker architecture model. This protocol has been designed to function with weaker networks where data loss and connection loss in between are frequent. It has been designed to function over TCP. MQTT has better adoption and wider library support when compared to CoAP.

- Constrained application protocol (CoAP)

CoAP also is a protocol optimized for Internet of things and this is from the IETF. It supports RESTful services and works based on client server approach. It can be used over UDP. The connectivity over firewalls and NAT networks are not simple when compared to the MQTT.

Both MQTT and CoAP have their own strengths and weaknesses and they are used according to the situations.

Enterprise Service Bus or Middleware Layer

There is a need for aggregation layer to consolidate and enable the communication among the brokers and other entities. This is the primary service bus, something like a backbone where everything is connected to each other. It is very significant in the architecture since it supports an HTTP server and MQTT broker to communicate with the devices. This layer has gateways to combine the communications from different devices and route them to appropriate destinations. They function as bridge among the different protocols for making communication possible from end to end. For instance, it supports HTTP based APIs and MQTT messages. Along with that, it also provides support to the legacy protocols. It also performs critical role in ensuring the security by enforcing the policies. Depends upon the Enterprise requirements the identity and access management will have various complexities and the middleware layer supports them to function.

Application management layer has responsibilities like event processing, information storage and data analytics.

On top of Enterprise service bus, the application management layer takes care of higher level application concerns. It should have the capability to handle data into databases and to process the events when they occur in the system. The application layer part of the Enterprise Architecture is the most versatile part where the developers have various technology choices to build their applications and databases. In most of the places, the amount of data and arrival of data is huge and they prefer support of a separate big data analytics platform. A cloud scalable platform lie Apache Hadoop provides very effective analytics such as map reduce. Event processing to manage the real time functionalities of the system also taken care by the application programs.

User Interface and External Communication Layer

The Enterprise application should provide well defined methods to communicate with the outside world. The external world includes various types of users with different access methods like smart phone application, web application, a kiosk or similar interface and external applications like web services which would communication with the enterprise application for integration or auditing purposes. Web based front ends are highly popular due to their access in any device with an internet connectivity. User groups can be created with different access permissions to work with the web based dash boards where the application programs render various analytics and information.

Any enterprise application can be made to talk with another application with the help of APIs. API management system also available in this layer which manages and controls the APIs. The API has to be continuously updated with newer versions and they have to be made available to the users. Several technologies such as Python, Ruby, PHP, Servlets/JSP are available to build the applications in the application tier. Smart phone applications are also getting popular due to their portability and availability of additional sensors.

5.3 Middleware Solutions for Enterprise IoT

Internet of Things Middleware is software that functions as an interface between components of the IoT, making communication possible among disparate elements that would not be naturally speaking with each other. IoT middleware deals with the structure, format and encoding of the information that is being exchanged between different layers, devices and sensors. It acts as a communication platform that interconnects variety of devices, sensors, protocols, operating systems and applications. Middleware is needed for integration before data can be analyzed [3].

Independent disconnected systems will create siloes of IoT ecosystems which will impact the agility and scalability of the whole system development. So the middleware design is very critical in end to end solution development. The functional components of the IoT middleware is illustrated in Fig. 5.1.

Middlware technologies are not just serving IoT applications. They are known for interconnecting different platforms from very early stages of software development. Beginning from Common Request Broker Architecture (CORBA), COM, DCOM there were several middlware solutions functioning in Enterprise Application Integration (EAI) space. The recent developments were web services which has made development and integration of Enterprise solutions without any dependency of platforms or languages or other technologies (Fig. 5.2).

The middleware plays a crucial role in development of application. API management is a critical function of middleware. Developers use to see everything in terms of programmatic calls to methods. It may be a physical device or a protocol or any interface, the middleware enables handling them in terms of simple API management [4].

The middleware tries to call APIs from disparate systems, taking care of interconnections. So it needs to be scalable and configurable. The middleware should support dynamic changes in the number of devices, amount of data or any higher level business requirements such as user managements and permissions. New sensor or device should automatically be inducted into the ecosystem.

Management of APIs along with other functions like routing, transformation and messaging also critical challenges to be solved by middleware designers.

Several proprietary middleware solutions are available now to build the Enterprise IoT systems. Mulesoft, Oracle, RedHat and WSO2 are among the companies that offer IoT middleware.

These products provide API management as well as basic messaging, routing and message transformation. More comprehensive IoT platforms include middleware along with sensors and networking components. The services provided by these middleware are different according to their specific scope and the Enterprises prefer to choose one of them according to their requirements [5].

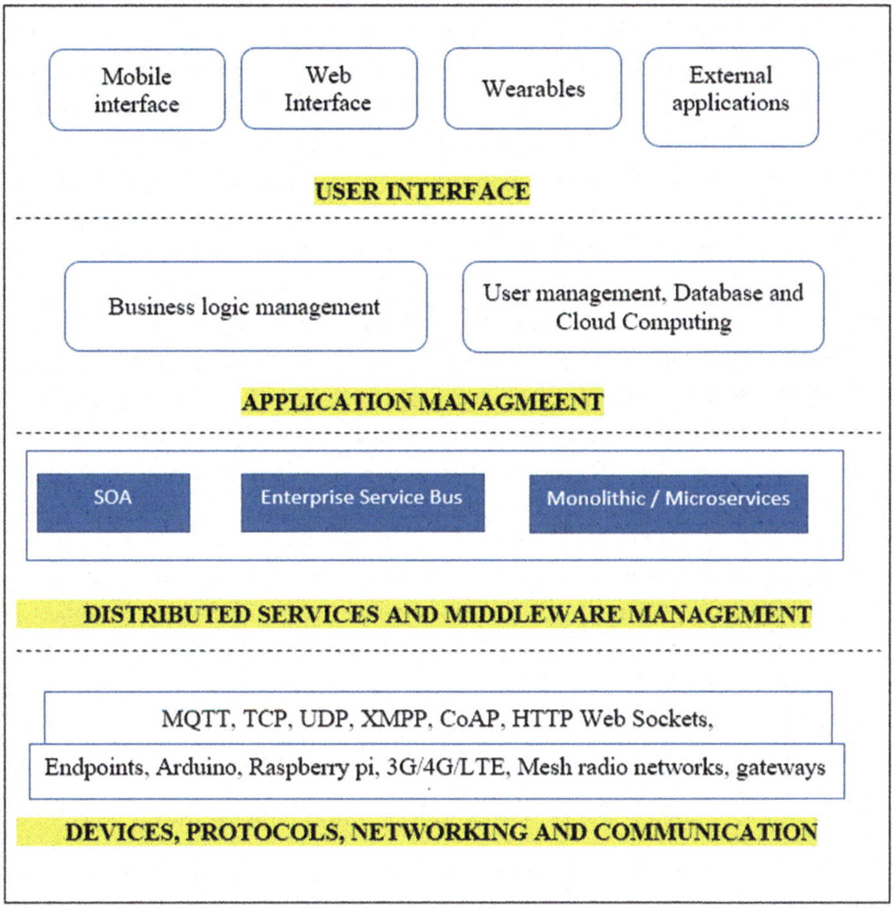

Fig. 5.1 A reference architecture for IoT

5.4 Monolithic Software Architectures

With the continuous development and evolvement of Internet of Things (IoT), Enterprise IoT applications become much larger in scale and even more complex in structure. This leads to poor scalability, extensibility and maintainability.

In the monolithic architecture software system is deployed as a single solution, in which functionally distinguishable aspects are all interwoven. The natural advantages of monolithic architecture are module independent, uniform standards and technology stack. Many researches offer solutions from perspective of monolithic architecture. Earlier IoT studies mainly focus on hardware network and low-level software technology (Fig. 5.3).

Monolithic architecture has some inevitable defects. First, the entire system is a united application; only multiple deployments can improve the system performance,

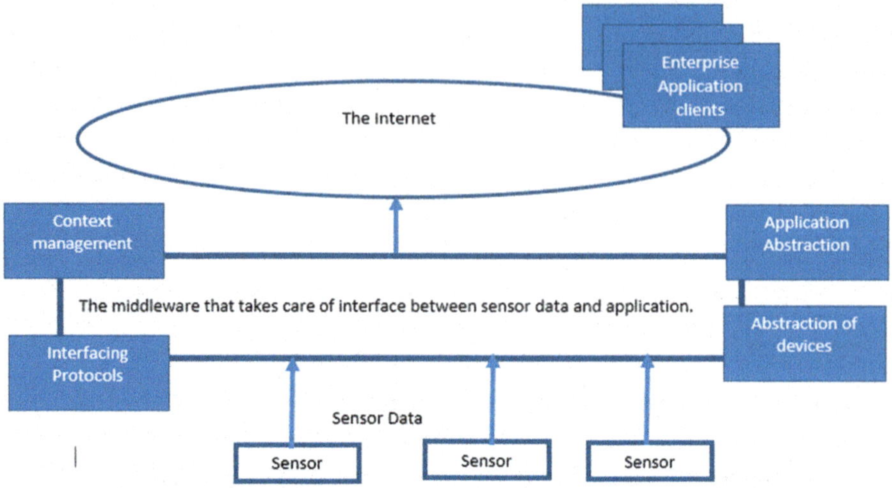

Fig. 5.2 Middleware functional components for Enterprise IoT

Fig. 5.3 Monolithic architecture of multi-tier application model

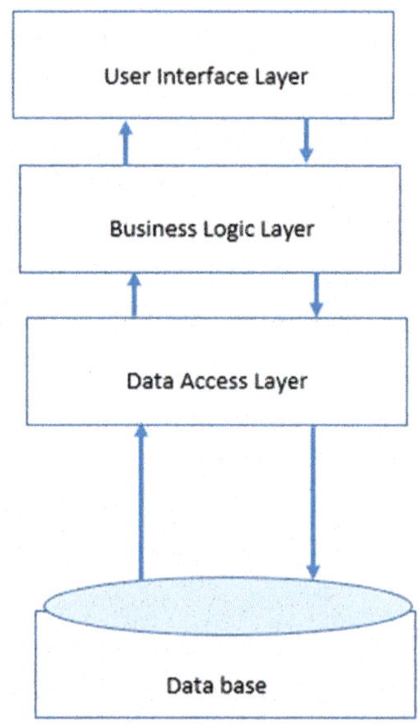

while the overloaded functions create bottleneck, which is a waste of computing resources. Second, in the case of the change and evolution of the system, a change in a function may affect other functions due to high dependencies. This also brings complexity for re-deployment, maintenance and continuous integration. Finally, the whole system uses a sole technology stack and development standards, which in turn limits the methods to solve the problem of physical heterogeneity.

5.5 Microservices Applications

Microservices describes a software architecture built around small, decoupled processes that communicate through language-agnostic APIs. The Microservices landscape is being influenced by the impact of mobile and Internet of Things (IoT), which increase the pressures to improve and accelerate software delivery. Microservices approach is a way of breaking down applications into manageable units of executables.

Instead of in-memory function calls, separate processes will be implemented. These are functionally atomic and highly decoupled and task specific. They communicate with each other using lightweight mechanisms like REST API.

Several prominent corporate have migrated to Microservices. Netflix, eBay, Amazon, Twitter, PayPal, Soundcloud are few of them. They have experienced immense benefits in terms of maintainability of their system and continuous development and integration.

In the field of IoT applications, Microservice architecture has been introduced in response to the challenges faced by monolithic applications. The primary merits considered were its flexibility, lightweight and loose coupling. It has better capacity to support interoperability and accommodate heterogeneous objects. In addition, this framework can easily achieve more application integration such as automation, intelligence, Geo service and Big Data (Fig. 5.4).

Microservice architecture is considered as a new software design pattern. It suggests that a single large and complex application should be divided into small manageable groups, where each group deals with the related services. According to its specific business responsibilities, each microservice is dedicated for a single business function. Any applicable tools and languages can quickly realize a specific service. Compared with the traditional monolithic architecture, the microservice architecture has obvious advantages, such as complexity under control, independent deployment, more choices for technology stack and fault tolerance, which will facilitate the development of IoT applications on large scale.

While data collected in the IoT generates billion pieces of information with hundreds of data formats, it's hard to classify vast amount of raw data by a complex module in traditional architecture, and it also easily leads to system overload if a large number of redundant data directly goes to the application layer. Scalability and continuous integration. IoT aims to keep on growing all the time and it has generated a lot of complex code. Developers with different technological skills often concern differently and everyone has their own limitations. So a good and independent architecture can offer a mechanism that the programmers can enjoy the freedom of coding with simplified integration In a nutshell, with the development of IoT technology, traditional architecture can't meet the requirements of heterogeneous, interoperable, customizable and scalable systems. To deal with above challenges, it is recommended to decompose the IoT system into Microservices to perform different kinds of tasks [6, 7].

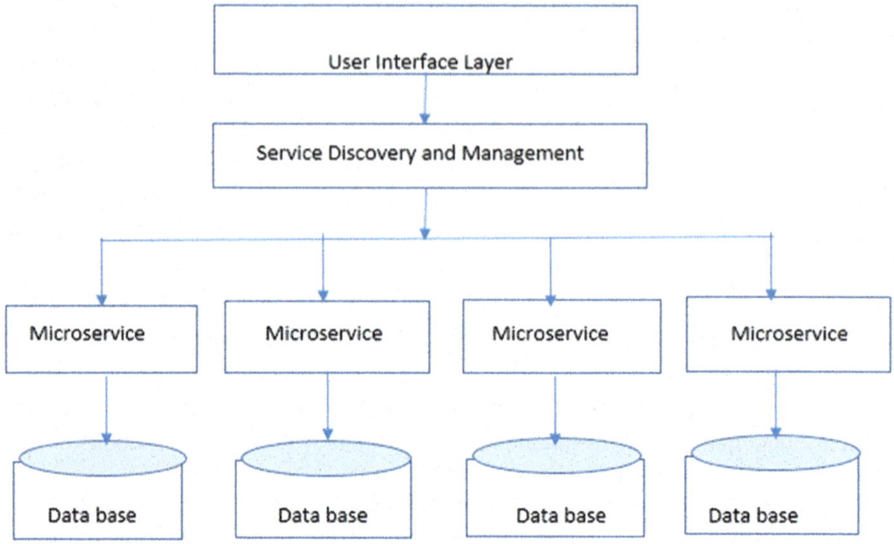

Fig. 5.4 Microservices model of an application

By using message driven and registry/discovery mechanism in core service, we can build systems that can easily extend, evolve and integrate third party applications to support interoperability and scalability. Moreover, the system uses device plugins to shield the differences of hardware facilities in order to support more heterogeneous platforms.

5.6 Enterprise IoT and Micro Services

Microservices are found suitable in the beginning for large scale Enterprise System development and there are many success stories, Similarly it is perfectly suitable for developing IoT Solutions of Enterprises too. Cloud-hosted Microservices would create an IoT model with less complexities. For example, one set of functions would speak to sensors and controllers and make them visible in the form of data rather than devices. The other set of functions could just process that data and apply some rules to that data. Yet another set of functions could fetch in data from third party enterprise systems like CRM/ERP systems. Thus, the very nature of IoT is supporting the architectural pattern of Microservices. Microservices also offer a way of scaling the infrastructure both horizontally and vertically giving long term benefits to the IoT deployments. Each of the services can scale based on the needs.

Given the dynamism of deployment and scalability expectations which comes with IoT, Microservices need to become an important part of the overall IoT Strategy [9].

The following characteristics of Microservices are seamlessly solve the challenges of Enterprise IoT.

Autonomy: Each component service in a microservices architecture can be developed, deployed, operated, and scaled without affecting the functioning of other services. The Enterprise Application Integration challenges were handled with web services which would bridge autonomous systems together which can solve a collective purpose. In IoT from edge to cloud there are several functional and technical requirements which can be composed by autonomous components using Microservices.

Specialized: Since there is no dependency among the services, each service is designed for a set of capabilities and focuses on solving a specific problem alone.

Agile: Microservices foster an organization of small, independent teams that take ownership of their services. It supports an Agile model of system development where the end product is developed by several iterations done by independent teams which is a fundamental requirement for Enterprise IoT.

Flexible: Enterprise IoT often experiences unpredictability in the demands of the system. Microservices allow each service to be independently scaled to meet demand for the application feature it supports.

Ease of Deployment: Microservices enable continuous integration and continuous delivery, making it easy to try out new ideas and to roll back if something doesn't work. It plays a major role in Devops practise where the development and operations need to be in sync. Quick deployment avoids delay in transforming the technology changes to operations.

Freedom: Teams have the freedom to choose the best tool to solve their specific problems. It is no longer necessary to stick with same set of technologies, platforms or tools throughout the application family for the sake of uniform communication. Microservices enables different business units of an Enterprise can have their own technology choice.

Resilience: Service independence increases an application's resistance to failure. When the success of Enterprise IoT systems are defined based on their up time and revenue generation, Resilience is a non-negotiable feature.

5.7 The Trade-Off Between Monolithic and Micro Services

When it is clearly understood that Companies that start investing in Microservices reap several benefits and their eco system changes very rapidly and move on further towards architectures like messaging, key value stores, and the kinds of things that facilitate communication and data sharing between services, there are down sides too. This may not be suitable to every company and it may be a difficult problem to solve in some environments to build a Microservices ecosystem [8].

It is easier to construct a monolithic systems since we don't have to worry about the problem of communication among the services and managing them throughout

Table 5.1 Comparison of monolithic and microservices approaches

	Monolithic	Micro services
1	Simple to develop, test and deploy in the early stages of any application development. It gets complicated while things becomes huge	From the early stages, it needs meticulous planning and design. It is not intended for very simple application development tasks
2	It has limitation in terms of size and complexity	Scalability is an important aspect in micro services and it adopts well when the application gets complicated
3	Need to redeploy the entire application on each update	Due to the independent deployments a huge time is saved without the need to redeploy the entire application
4	Continuous deployment is difficult	It is designed for continuous deployment.
5	Reliability is lesser. Bug in a module can bring down the entire application	The bugs like memory leaks can be effectively isolated and treated
6	New technologies cannot be adopted because of the integration challenges. So there are constraints in terms of choosing the development technology	Complete freedom can be experienced in terms of technology selection for a service. As they are deployed separately the services can talk to each other and the development teams have their freedom to choose the most effective technology stack for a particular service
7	Database operations are comparatively simpler due to the centralized database of a monolithic architecture	Microservices has the partitioned database architecture. Business transactions that update multiple business entities in a microservices-based application need to update multiple databases owned by different services. Using distributed transactions is usually not an option and you end up having to use an eventual consistency based approach, which is more challenging for developers

the application life cycle. When two different functionalities of a same system is running in two separate processes, in two separate containers, in separate virtual machines, we must worry about data coordination. So, there are definitely some overheads that we must solve as a result of choosing to go with Microservices.

So the Enterprises should make a decision based on the challenges to be faced while implementing Microservices. Some of the challenges are comparatively trivial or easily handled, whereas others may require new processes or tools for the company. Some of the challenges are given in this section.

Microservices can be less stable than when it gets complex and huge. An individual Microservice can be well-tested before deployment in conjunction with some common configurations and programs, it's practically impossible to test every configuration of Microservices in the real world scenario. As we combine them, they may interact in unforeseen ways.

Security in containers can be an issue. It's not always easy to tell where Microservices reside, which can make securing them a headache. And with different Microservices interacting with each other, this gives hackers more opportunities to penetrate the system. Experienced DevOps teams are moving to a more granular security policy called microsegmentation to get around this problem — but the solution isn't universal yet.

The migration from Monolithic to Microservices is a difficult process and the Enterprises should make a judgement to check if the investment is worth for it. It can be difficult to make the transition. If a company has been producing and maintaining a monolithic application, it will take time and discipline to replace it with a micro services architecture – although many companies have successfully accomplished this, and found the investment worthwhile.

As a summary, the following table provides a comparative study of Monolithic and Microservices architecture (Table 5.1).

This chapter introduces the idea of Enterprise IoT with all its challenges and possibilities. The consumer IoT cannot be expected to reward in proportion with the amount of Research and Development...

5.8 Conclusion

This chapter discussed various architectural concerns in the Enteprise IoT solution. It is important to understand various components in an Enterprise IoT solution before the design and implementation phase which is discussed in the next chapter. The software architectural choices and the middleware layer concerns are highly critical in the process of understanding the Enterprise IoT solution. The differences between monolith architectures and microservices architectures have been discussed beyond a software engineering perspective and with respect to the Enterprise IoT context. The readers are provided with a comprehensive analysis about the tradoff between both the architectures which will help them to make a decision about their architecture before step into other phases of development.

References

1. Gubbi J et al (2013) Internet of Things (IoT): a vision, architectural elements, and future directions. Future Generation Comput Syst:1645–1660
2. Zhou J et al (2013) CloudThings: a common architecture for integrating the internet of things with cloud computing. Huazhong University of Science and Technology, Wuhan
3. Jarwar MA, Kibria MG, Ali S, Chong I (2018) Microservices in web objects enabled IoT environment for enhancing reusability. Sensors (Basel, Switzerland) 18(2):352. https://doi.org/10.3390/s18020352
4. Bandyopadhyay S, Sengupta M, Maiti S, Dutta S (2011) Role of Middleware for Internet of Things: a study. Int J Comput Sci Eng Survey (IJCSES) 2(3)
5. Arthur de M. Del Esposte, Kon F, Costa FM, Lago N (2017) InterSCity: a scalable microservice-based open source platform for smart cities. In: Published at 6th international conference on Smart cities and Green ICT, Portugal, April, 2017

6. Shadija D, Rezai M, Hill R (2017, December). Microservices: granularity vs. performance. In: Proceedings of the10th international conference on utility and cloud computing, Austin, Texas, USA—December 05–08, 2017, pp 215–220
7. Pahl C, Jamshidi P (2016) Microservices: a systematic mapping study, pp 137–146. https://doi.org/10.5220/0005785501370146
8. Heinrich R, van Hoorn A, Knoche H, Li F, Lwakatare LE, Pahl C, Schulte S, Wettinger J (2017) Performance engineering for microservices: research challenges and directions. https://doi.org/10.1145/3053600.3053653
9. https://www.digitalistmag.com

Chapter 6
Design and Implementation of Enterprise IoT Solutions

Abstract Design and implementation of any engineering project would require plenty of careful planning and estimation. Especially Enterprise IoT projects have more challenges due to the involvement of multi-disciplinary challenges. This chapter tries to address the important concerns in initiating the implementation activity of an Enterprise IoT project. This chapter does not address the technicalities of implementation or the design procedure, but the higher level requirements for commencing the implementation. The use case development and technology choices for hardware and software are discussed in detail. There are several vendors who are manufacturing hardware devices for the Enterprise IoT solutions. They support various protocols and behave differently when it comes to data collection and management. Similarly, the software stack also very fragmented in nature. From the edge computing to cloud computing there are several options which are to be analyzed and chosen carefully. The implementation scope goes beyond simple data collection and basic processing. The technology landscape is dominated by few emerging trends which are changing the Enterprise works. The last part of this chapter discusses three major technology breakthroughs which needs to be considered while implementation is done. Big data analytics and Artificial Intelligence are gaining momentum in the development world nowadays. The algorithms and other basic concepts of Artificial Intelligence or machine learning were developed long ago. However only now we are able to get the large amount of data due to Enterprise IoT to experience the benefits of those algorithms. The Block chain technology is another game changer in the data management space. It has huge promises for security, immutability and other characteristics of data which have been desired for long. These latest advancements have been discussed in the last part of the chapter.

Keywords Bigdata for IoT · AI in IoT · Machine learning and IoT · Block chain for IoT · Enterprise IoT design · Enterprise IoT implementation

L. S. Jayashree, G. Selvakumar, *Getting Started with Enterprise Internet of Things: Design Approaches and Software Architecture Models*,
https://doi.org/10.1007/978-3-030-30945-9_6

Learning Objectives

1. To learn the basic design requirements for Enterprise IoT
2. To understand the various constraints in designing and implementing the Enterprise IoT solution.
3. To learn how the recent technology advancements can be incorporated to Enterprise IoT applications.

6.1 Introduction

Agencies like Gartner are coming up with data that explains how IoT technology is transforming the operations and how fast the adoption of IoT in enterprises. With the appropriate hardware, connectivity, software and proper usage of protocols and applications Enterprises are continuously innovating in their business areas. When it comes to design and implementation of Enterprise IoT, the role of all stakeholders including the end users, technical architects, business analysis and developers are very significant. The ultimate objective of rolling out IoT enabled system is to cut down expenses, develop new revenue streams and gain better control over the enterprise. To achieve all these objectives maximum care has to be shown from the design phase by understanding all the challenges and following up all the guidelines. There are several failure projects in Enterprises due to their ignorance in allotting time to understand the problem fully and making a fool proof design. Adequate analysis and research activities are extremely important before starting the design and implementation phases. The guidelines and standards are slowly evolving, and the Enterprises should be keen on learning those best practices for design and implementation of IoT.

6.2 Critical Design Goals of Enterprise IoT

When we attempt to develop solutions for Enterprise IoT, the design phase has certain unique challenges when compared to non-enterprise solutions. Here is a list of some important design goals that needs to be considered while IoT solutions are developed for Enterprises [5].

- Interoperability among various commercial entities
- Scalability
- Precision and Accuracy
- Programmability
- Resilience
- Serviceability

Interoperability
Industrial IoT solutions are introduced by different commercial entities according to their own technology convenience and business strategies. When they want to collaborate and work interoperability should be ensured. During the design phase this factor should be considered. Also the IoT solutions developed should co-exist in an environment with a significant amount of legacy operations technologies (OT), including SCADA, M2M, and other manufacturing execution systems. Industrial IoT solutions must integrate, support various protocols and data sets, and work reliably with these manufacturing systems. Equally important, IIoT solutions must integrate with back-office enterprise resource planning (ERP) systems.

Scalability
The major requirement for Industrial IoT solutions is the ability to scale seamlessly when the demand grows. Industrial networks are specialized large scale networks and usually consists of tens of thousands of controllers, robots, machinery, and other purpose built applications. They should be able to support addition of tens of thousands of new sensors, devices and controllers whenever required. This process of scaling up the system should not be hindering the other processes and should happen as seamlessly as possible.

Precision and Accuracy
The required accuracy at which synchronization among different processes is usually in terms of milliseconds in commercial solutions. For better quality, Enterprises should deploy very effective quality assurance systems which can detect minute variations in the parameters monitored and take immediate corrective actions based on those measurements. A very small downtime could make a huge impact on the good will and revenues of the company.

Programmability
In industrial scenario, we may not be able to predict the requirements for new changes. The systems should handle the situations where they need to be frequently reprogrammed and reconfigured to support new processes. This programming is done remotely, on site or in the field. Every layer in the IoT architecture is undergoing rapid developments. The interface to the user or to the other layers are becoming more programmable and API driven. The design of Industrial IoT solutions should consider this as an important design goal and ensure that the design is appropriate for programmable customizations in the future.

Resilience
System failure is not an option in several mission critical processes where even a millisecond down time could be very expensive. They should be designed by keeping resilience as an important design goal. Suitable backup systems should be designed from the beginning itself to ensure the operations are not stopped because of a failure in one part of the system. From a loss of sensors to a loss of connectivity, industrial IoT systems and architectures must compensate for in-use failures, and still be able to satisfactorily complete its processes and operations.

Serviceability
Industrial systems must operate reliably and predictably in harsh conditions for years and years. Supporting this level of performance requires regular maintenance from in-house and field service technicians. IoT solutions operating in industrial environments must be serviceable in order to sustain the levels of performance required. From swapping out sensors, updating firmware, to configuring gateways and servers, the ability to maintain industrial IoT solutions over its entire lifecycle is an essential requirement.

6.3 The Concerns of Enterprise IoT Design and Implementation

6.3.1 Hardware Related Concerns

When we start designing the Enterprise IoT design, the first thing that we need to understand is the kind of sensors and other hardware devices which are appropriate for the data that we are planning to collect. Since it is going to play a vital role in budget related estimations, the Enterprises should pay more attention on choosing suitable hardware according to the requirements. The environmental conditions are to studied carefully before choosing the devices. If the place is subjected to undergo high pressure water for cleaning or hot steam, then a complete different set of devices with special ratings need to be chosen for the design. The sensor endpoints may be required to be placed within perfect enclosures which may need special fittings on the infrastructure. If devices get unplugged or get broken it will be a serious issue. So necessary protective mechanism should be there. Battery replacement is another significant concern when we design the hardware layer. Enterprise IoT endpoints are typically installed with batteries of 5 year life time or more. However, an intelligent strategy is required to change the batteries whenever required. The devices and placement of devices has to be chosen according this factor. In the design there must be facilities to know the battery levels of the endpoints and there must be an automated alert mechanism when the battery levels goes down beyond a level. It may be challenging when the assets or on the move, such as ships with sensors attached with containers for various monitoring purposes. It may not be possible to proceed any maintenance activity in the middle of the sea. So the devices has to be chosen according to the requirement very carefully. Another significant concern is updating the firmware whenever required to ensure that the security requirements are met all the time.

6.3.2 Networking Concerns

The network communication in Enterprise IoT is always a trickier one when the cluster of sensor endpoints are connected to the gateways in the premises of the enterprises. The infrastructure usually causes problems like attenuation and interference to weaken and distort the signals. Wi-Fi and Bluetooth can deliver very short-range communications considering many of the enterprise applications. Bluetooth BLE, ZigBee and S-Wave mesh technologies are being used for building more stable sensor networks in enterprise IoT market. At present LoRaWAN and few proprietary 900 MHz based systems are the best choices for enterprise scale IoT. They deliver very good range of communication which is more than 6 miles with high reliability in almost all the environments [6].

6.3.3 Data Concerns

During the design phase, the nature of data to be handled in the Enterprise impacts several decisions. The data from a single sensor to the gateway may be as modest as 50 bytes. When we consider the total data transmission from all the endpoints of a business unit, say around 5000 sensors will be huge. Moreover, when the frequency of data transmission is shorter i.e., every 2 min the usage of bandwidth will be more. So, in the design phase the enterprises should carefully decide the most significant data to be collected which has meaningful impact on the decision making or analytics or any higher-level process. Most of the enterprises experience this as a problem in the due course of implementation, that major portion of the data collected from end points are not used meaningfully anywhere in the system.

6.3.4 Programming and Backend Concerns

Already backend as services have become so popular and in the IoT era, they are getting more attention. In the design phase, the time and effort estimation will happen, and the programming and backend components will be chosen according to the complexity of the project, deadlines, budget, available skill set and other similar factors. Bugs in the backend services are major showstoppers in many of the Enterprise IoT deployments. However, the programming technologies and the backend for data processing are heavily depend upon the architecture chosen for the enterprise IoT solution. We have dealt with the various architectural aspects in the previous chapter. During the implementation phase, the development of an application program interface (API) is a critical element. API allows how the communication takes place with the external applications through message calls.

6.4 Enterprise IoT Implementation Guidelines

6.4.1 *Determining the Larger Vision and Mission*

The planning is the corner stone for any successful IoT project development. It starts with creating a vision for the enterprise and drafting a step by step procedure to develop and deploy the entire application. Before developing a feasible implementation strategy, the administrators should ensure that all the use cases have been thoroughly brain stormed and incorporating IoT in those selected or entire set of workflows are recommended. Because backtracking may not be very economical in Enterprise IoT projects. Few fundamental things to be done in the due course of designing an Enterprise IoT.

Developing the vision and mission statements for the Enterprise IoT project is the very basic and fundamental step needs to be completed in the beginning. The operational benefits experienced by the companies and the value propositions delivered by cyber physical systems are numerous. Performing a case study on those previously built systems and to understand the similarities and differences with the Enterprise in consideration. To begin with, the managerial team should start with asking a very important set of key questions about the initiative. The questions may differ from organization to organization. However, the following are some of the common facts to be learnt from the answers of the questions [5].

- The opportunities for automation in various business processes and workflows in the entire Enterprise
- Those opportunities that can be mapped to the business problems of the organization
- The scope of solution space. Ie., IoT can be used for Tracking the assets, remote monitoring or preventive maintenance.
- The initial and recurring cost for each use case and the monetary benefit if the implementation is successful.
- The technology choices for the implementation and the skill set availability.
- Identification of major stakeholders including the multiple domain team leaders and partners to implement the solution.
- The scope for sustainability and scalability in future.

The above questions must be asked to select individuals from various teams. The collective answers for the above questions provide the vision and mission of the IoT initiative. The above facts also provide the insight about the size of the project, complexity of the tasks to be done, skill gaps to be filled up, estimations to be done etc.,

6.4.2 Identification of Use Cases and Requirements

The importance of clearly defining problem statement has been emphasized more than anything in the development of any technical domain. The success of an IoT initiative in the Enterprise is largely depends upon the clarity of use cases defined. The use cases and the key success metrics has to be defined clearly ahead of design and implementation. Due to time constraints and other limitations, early implementation may be started in few occasions which is too risky. The consequences of implementing the use cases like the impact in productivity and improvement in efficiency has to be documented for long run. This metrics will provide guidelines for the implementation process. Instead of audacious goals, the enterprises should plan their implementation plan from small and quantifiable modules to bigger ones. Due to the relative newness in the domain, there may not be enough track records or experiences which can be helpful in case of stumbling blocks. In case of a large commercial fleet or logistics company the implementation may start first by locating the fleet on the move efficiently and in next stage to optimize the routes. In the consequent versions, they could implement the modules for more elaborate objectives like maximizing the utilization, saving time and fuel, proactively avoiding flat tires, oil loss, waiting time in the tolls, frequency of sudden breaks, scheduling loading and unloading etc., IoT has all the potential to supply enough data for all these operations.

6.4.3 Technology Stack Identification

In Enterprise IoT environments massive datasets are generated from the end points of different types and a variety of connectivity mechanisms and protocols are used in the system along with various choices for hardware and software choices. During the design and implementation phase, the appropriate technology stack should be identified by carefully analysing all the merits and demerits.

The IoT stack is continuously growing and maturing into a separate set of layers and each layers needs to communicate with the other layers for better integration. As the technology stack is clearly defined for the Enterprise, it will be easier for the developers to create the services and functionalities based on them. Basically, the following are the common layers where the technology choices are spread across for the Enterprise IoT.

- Sensors
  - Sensors are the devices which are close to the physical environment to capture the data from the real world.
  - Sensors have become common after the popularity of smartphones which comes with inbuilt sensors for observing various physical parameters. The enterprises are coming up with new products where thousands of new device

are connected to the internet to exchange information about the physical world which is captured by the sensors. They are relatively very small and inexpensive and can be used with almost all the devices exist in the industry. They can be even connected to the smartphone vis Bluetooth and it can be used to communicate with the internet.
  - All the above layers are flooded with new solutions and technologies and they are emerging rapidly. Because, the use cases, applications, nature of data, functional and non functional requirements are not the same across all the industries. They have different price points, speed and power requirements, networking limitations and other deciding factors. A smart meter in a wind mill and smart health monitor in a hospital are going to be implemented completely in a different manner.
  - The application designing team of the Enterprise should review each use case, device requirements and other constraints in each layer, they will come to better decision about the technologies.
  - Nowadays sensors are even embedded in watches, contact lenses, wristbands, and fabrics. Companies are working on sensors on tattoos also which causes vibration to alert. The alert can be programmed for various events. University of Washington, Microsoft, Nokia and several other companies are working on that. There is a very large spectrum in the quality of sensors and other devices which makes selecting the hardware a challenging one.

- Microcontrollers
  - Microcontrollers do the basic decision making of what is to be done with the data collected. It takes care of local storage, data processing and internet connectivity to the unit.
  - The collected data is normally so huge and the entire data is not required to be sent to the cloud. There are actions like analysing, extracting, cleaning and consolidating the collected data before sending them to the backend. The volume has to be reduced to avoid unnecessary traffic to the cloud and to save the storage costs. The microcontroller is responsible for all this. The popular micro controller devices are Arduino and Raspberry pi. The microcontroller devices have variations like programmable microcontrollers which enables taking actions like switching something on or off, opening or closing a valve etc., These should be well understood before we make the decision of hardware check list for implementation.

- Connectivity
  - Another significant aspect to be inspected in this layer is the capability to network. Because the data obtained from the devices has to be sent to the cloud.
  - It may be wireless or wired. Wired networks are adequate for the stationary devices with nearby power sources. However, there must be clear estimation about the number of wired and wireless network requirements. Most of the situations require wireless connections, since wired networking does not

make much sense in any enterprise eco system. It increases the complexity if there is shortage of space and other constraints. Another decision to be made here is capacity of batteries. In some cases, continuous connectivity is required. In several cases collecting the data by batches and updating them on frequent intervals may be enough. The battery and connectivity arrangements should be according to that.

- Internet service platforms
  - The end to end experience of the IoT product or the use case realization is happening only with the help of internet service platform.
  - The service platform layer serves the purpose for the end user. It communicates to the customers by delivering the analytics done and the insights obtained. This layer responsible for the business value of the application.
  - A separate chapter is dedicated to discuss various IoT platforms and how to select an appropriate one. Here we just look at some of the essential elements of Internet service platforms.
  - In most of the cases the service platforms function on the cloud and it is utilized as a software as a service. The Enterprise should decide appropriate storage and bandwidth requirements for the services platform. However, since they will be deployed in the cloud, scalability will not be an issue except the budget allocated for the cloud services [4].

6.5 Recent Value Additions in Enterprise IoT Implementation

6.5.1 Big Data and Analytics

Data analytics plays a major role in the Enterprise which turns out the raw data from the hardware device layer to valuable data by subjecting it to some processing. The outcome of analytics will be some statistics or patterns or in the form of trends which helps the organizations to make effective decisions in short, medium or longer terms. Beyond Internet of Things, Big data analytics is getting much popularity nowadays. Big data analytics is becoming more of a necessity than an optional nowadays due to the enormous amount of data generated by the endpoints and due to the complicated business decisions and actions to be made on the real time. This section addresses some of the concerns to be taken care of while we deal with big data analytics with IoT implementation [3].

Reference Data

The implementation of Enterprise IoT will become meaningful when the right context is applied on the data collected by all the endpoints. However, collecting the data alone will not serve the purpose. There must be a well-defined analysis process to obtain the insights required for Enterprise. For that the first requirement is the context has to be set to the collected data with the help of reference datasets. The reference data sets have to be prepared from the historical records and sample data from which the context will be developed. If we get latitude and longitude data from a connected car, it needs to be understood as a location name, nearest city and all the meaningful information. If the signals are for a break down alert, the nearby service centres should get be notified. In this scenario, the reference data set is the database of customer service workshops which is mapped with GPS data. Similarly, for any meaningful action or insight the reference data set has to be prepared well. Data scientists and engineers will generate the reference data sets and mapping of data with atmost care to make the analytics more impactful.

Advanced Analytics with Machine Learning

Problem areas like predictive analytics can be handled with Machine learning algorithms for more accurate results. Every enterprise may not need machine learning; however, it is becoming a more powerful tool in several modern enterprise problems. So, in the process of planning, the Enterprises will ensure that professionals who have expertise in advanced analytics and machine learning are part of the implementation team.

Real Time Analytics or Streaming Analytics

More than analyzing data in a later point of time, performing real time analytics is becoming a critical requirement in several industries for safety and quality control reasons. Shutting down a gas refilling machine after detecting an inappropriate pressure needs to be done spontaneously. The abnormality should be detected within milliseconds and the action should be taken immediately within milliseconds by a standing instruction or rule. The real time analytics is more critical in healthcare organizations where the statistics of hundreds of patients are observed through the IoT enabled systems and proper alerts are to be generated. Hot path analytics is the common term used to refer the process where a pipeline or a buffer is used to which the data is routed to make the real time analytics. During the development process, the architects need to determine the important data should be sent for hot path analytics.

Implementation of Cold Path Analytics

Another style of data analytics which is opposite to the hot path analytics which was discussed just above is the cold path analytics where data analytics is done as batch processing and it is a long-term analytics methodology. Here a set of data collected from the sensors, aggregated, processed and analyzed to create insights and reports which can be used for longer term which is not necessarily required at the same time of data collection. Analyzing power consumption data in a smart city to make peak time estimations is a typical example for cold path analytics.

Separating the data points according to their requirement for cold path analytics is an essential during the development process.

Other Analytics with IoT Implementation

Smart parking applications are getting much attention in modern cities and they come under spatial analytics. Here the relationship between the spatial location and the physical objects are continuously monitored and analyzed. Location based IoT applications are primarily making use of spatial analytics. Another usual requirement is to analyze the trends and patterns based on time which is known as time series analytics. Weather forecasting, smart agriculture and health monitoring applications would benefit from this kind of analytics. To determine the best step of actions in a situation can be the outcome of prescriptive analysis which is the combination of descriptive and predictive analytics.

During the implementation of Enterprise IoT solution, the architects should consider all the possibilities and requirements for the various analytics.

A product can be monitored not only during the manufacturing process, but throughout it's life time. The sensors can be positioned in the products ranging from huge industrial equipments to house hold appliances which keep on communicating with their manufacturers. The manufacturers collect the data for making maintenance in a predictive manner and to market suitable spare parts and accessories. It increases the safety and surveillance of an Enterprise through video sensors available.

Thus the implementation of advanced analytics techniques with IoT in an Enterprise should be promoted to improve the revenues, The utilization of data analytics shall, therefore, be promoted in the area of IoT to gain improved revenue, customer engagement and satisfaction, follow up of product usage and competitive gain.

Artificial Intelligence

It has been a common phenomenon to live and work the virtual assistants like Siri or Alexa or google assistant. They are becoming a part of our life slowly by enriching their capabilities. Slowly it is becoming possible that we can ask Alexa to order food delivery at door with careful description about the preparation of dishes. The washing machine and TV can function with more intelligence to understand our schedules, atmosphere, our mood and other similar parameters. Google assistant has even come up with a voice assistant which can make a phone call to a business on behalf of the owner and it can book appointments or order things which is expected to be available in the market shortly.

All these advancements are achieved with the help of Artificial Intelligence which is getting more focus nowadays due to the increased processing power of our computers and the huge availability of data. Naturally, Artificial intelligence can be applied to several use cases of Enterprise IoT where the availability of data is abundant and decision making is crucial with the data which is also challenging. For instance, in the cases of IoT enabled manufacturing streaming analytics needs to be done to reduce faulty products. Analysing uncountable patterns of data and inferring about the health of the output product can be achieved only by Artificial Intelligence enabled system with more accuracy.

Another example where the combination of AI and IoT is immensely obvious is the self driving cars. They are all connected and they have huge amount of data about the traffic, GPS location, routs etc., By using all these, the cars should take decision about the route to be taken, optimal speed and other things. The entire functionality is implemented using Artificial Intelligence.

Smart thermostat solutions by Nest Labs which has been recently acquired by Google is another good example where enterprises combine AI and IoT to build better environments. Here the smartphone is integrated with the system and the temperature is controlled based on the users' preferences and work schedule. This can be applicable for huge retail markets, shopping complexes and several other places.

New opportunities and markets like the above examples are rapidly growing and providing huge value to the enterprises. So, the enterprise architects should ensure that the implementation team has enough engineers with expertise in machine learning and artificial intelligence.

- Better customer satisfaction by voice assistance and more understanding of customers' problems
- Improved risk management by assessing and predicting the riskier situations with more accuracy eg., credit card or loan approval for customers. also in the manufacturing sector, it has been observed that the unplanned downtime can be reduced a lot with the help of appl
- Efficient and more optimized operations in the Enterprises such as controlling cooling operations of a data centre and effective supply chain decision making
- Technologies like computer vision, speech recognition and natural language processing helps to extract insight from different formats of data without any human review.
- Integrating AI enables development of new products and services. Natural language processing makes it possible to interact with the machines more naturally and the products like Drones and robots are employed in industrial sector for revolutionary business use cases.

Traditional approaches of analysing the structed data is slowly becoming out of scope due to vast amounts of real-time data streaming from IoT end points. The AI and ML based analysis makes the entire process more effective both in real time analytics as well as post event processing. Due to all the above advantages vendors of ioT platforms like Amazon, IBM, Microsoft, Oracle, PTC and GE are releasing their products with AI capabilities integrated.

6.5.2 Block Chain

Empowering IoT Applications with Block Chain

Internet of Things and Block chain are two disruptive technologies which are revolutionizing two different areas of interest. While Block chain can be seen as a distributed data model with unconventional control, Internet of Things is a broader hardware and software solution. We are attempting to bring both of them together to enhance the applications of both in the real world.

The strength of Block chain technology is the security provided by its design. Security is the biggest challenge faced by Internet of Things. Decentralization of data ownership, immutable data and transparency of data are the much required features of IoT solutions. Apart from security, Block chain helps IoT solutions to scale by adding more devices without worrying about new and complicated security policies [1].

On the other hand, by combining with IoT, Block chain will be considered in a larger landscape beyond the cryptocurrencies. Most of the enterprises consider the Block chain as something related to Bit coins and they fail to explore the possibilities of Block chain in the industrial sector. IoT provides natures ways of expanding the utilization of Block chain apart from cryptocurrencies.

The company which tries to utilize the combination of Block chain and IoT should consider some important aspects. The Block chain applications demand high performance computing infrastructure and it requires a talent pool with latest skill sets to tackle the complicated development process. The objectives of using Block chain has to be clearly defined in the first part. Because deploying a technology like Block chain is more time consuming and expensive. Without calculation of return on investments, it may not be advisable. Moreover, the company should have adequate capabilities to store and process huge amounts of data and abilities to work with the latest technologies like Artificial intelligence and Machine learning.

When IoT applications are becoming more significant in terms of contracts between different parties, the Block chain technology assures the peer to peer contracts and agreements without the requirement for any third party certification agency. Due to this the challenges like single point of failure and reliability can be handled very effectively.

Challenges and Opportunities

Though the consequences of merging Block chain with IoT are very promising, the execution is not simple and straightforward. There are few critical challenges to be addressed as given in this section.

Intensive Computational and Bandwidth Requirements

The devices in the IoT eco system are light weight in terms of their computational power and the resource availability. We need to find out alternative solutions to make the intensive computations for Block chain. Moreover, the processing time and power requirement for cryptographic calculations are also beyond the level. The types of IoT devices are very diverse and we may not be able to expect that devices of all the ranges can have the same computational power. Moreover, in Block chain networks data is not stored in centralized server. When the data becomes huge, it will be a big challenge to the decentralized network. The traffic created by Block chain protocols are not suitable for IoT networks where the bandwidth is very limited.

Scalability and Risk Management

Adding new nodes in the Block chain is not simple. However, IoT networks are known for large number of nodes, even in terms of thousands. It is not a desirable situation to effectively implement the Block chain for IoT. The Block chain is known for its decentralized record management. The nodes in IoT network may not be able to contain the data while the network grows over time. It may require centralization of data management when the network goes beyond certain level. It would compromise some of the benefits of Block chain.

The implementation of Block chain network in any organization needs an exclusive team with required expertise to design and deploy the system. Otherwise they need to reach out for block chain vendors in the market. Block chain as a service market is still in its early stages. Selecting the vendor suitable for the organization's culture and expectations is a riskier one. Even though Block chain technology is synonymous with security, the access level decides the ultimate security of a network. While a public block chain based system has a compromise on the private keys of any user, it may introduce false entries in the ledger.

Challenges in Implementation

The implementation of block chain in IoT requires several agreements between various players in the system. When the stockholders belong to different countries the legal and compliance demands also to be met. Moreover, the skill required to implement and maintain the entire stack of application is also a challenge when the technologies like block chain come into picture.

Discussion on Appropriate Use Cases

Whenever new set of technologies are introduced, it is very challenging to determine the appropriate real time scenarios in which the usage of those technologies make significant positive impacts. When the technologies are used just for the sake of utilizing an emerging trend, there would be plenty of bottle necks and other practical problems which would adversely affect the business requirements. So here we have handpicked few use cases where the combination of Internet of things and block chain are perfect partners in solving current business problems as well as providing assurance for future innovations [2].

Shared Economy Applications

The combination of IoT and block chain are most suitable for the shared economy applications where people and businesses come together in a decentralised environment such as Airbnb and exploit the opportunities of digital economy. In shared economy applications, people monetize what they have. Peer to peer automatic payment systems, management of digital rights, exchange of foreign money or bonds can be few applications which are going to be influenced by the block chain and IoT integration.

Peer to peer automatic payment systems, unconventional platforms for foreign exchanges are slowly getting attention due to the integration. We could see the rice of decentralized and autonomous applications - shortly known as Dapps. The existing buildings, house hold equipment, other devices and vehicles can become part of Dapps by adding a sensor and network connection. By introducing block chain, we can achieve transactions without a trusted third party by allowing our applications to function in a decentralised peer to peer mode. Already we have implementations

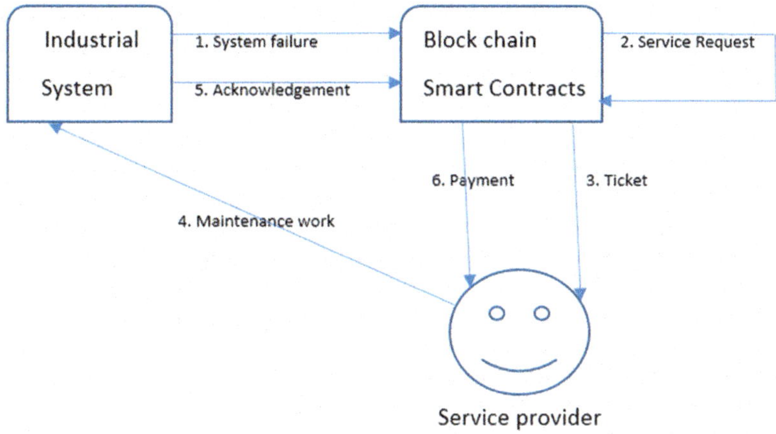

Fig. 6.1 Smart contracts with IoT

in usage such as Slock, where a property or any unused asset can be linked to block chain and it can be monetized with the help of a DApp (Decentralized Application).

The shared economy applications can be implemented in numerous scenarios including shared taxies, Airbnb, supply chain and similar domains. Fig. 6.1 illustrates a simple applications where a manufacturing industry has agreement with a service provider for maintenance work or repair work. The entire life cycle of maintenance can be automated with the help of IoT and block chain.

Smart contracts enable credible transactions without the need for an authorization agency. These contracts are irreversible and easily trackable. They provide security which is more reliable than the conventional method of transactions. In many occasions the transaction cost is comparatively lesser.

Whenever there is a requirement for the service, the automated system in the company creates a service request and it is sent to the service provider for taking necessary action. All communications are registered in the block chain as smart contracts which cannot be tampered. Thus, it results a smooth and reliable operations which are completely automated and precise.

Supply Chain Management

Supply chain management is a complicated domain where several stakeholders participate from different places of their business. Collaboration and communication between raw material suppliers, product manufacturers, logistics companies, shipments, retailers and customers is crucial to increase the transparency of supply chain life cycle. To prevent losses and delays the data collected from all the stages, starting from when the order is dispatched until the end-of-life of the product is significant. Getting the real-time visibility of the location and condition of shipments is a primary factor which decides the effectiveness of supply chains and the revenue of the companies. However, it has been immensely challenging to get all these data on time to make the business more profitable and to reduce the losses.

The contracts and rules exchanged among the different parties are the essential components of supply chain services. They are signed before the operation begins. Once the shipping started, parties like shipping agency, ports, custom officials, carriers and other entities take part in the execution. At each level, set of acknowledgements, messages, receipts are exchanged. This long chain of data is well suited for making use of Block chain to register all the transactions in between to ensure reliable, data driven and smooth process. The distributed ledger will be verified by the customers, logistics providers and government authorities anytime to obtain reliable information and to have better control over the entire supply chain and logistics domain.

Smart city Applications.

Smart city is a domain where plenty of smart solutions including smart infra structures, smart buildings are part of. In smart buildings, the information from sensors and control information from authorized users are sent to a centralized server and directed for appropriate device. In smart houses the house hold devices like refrigerators, dish washers, lights and security systems like alarms, cameras and locks are present. All these devices can be connected to the internet and controlled by Internet. Ensuring reliability and prevent intrusion are biggest challenges in this problem space. Because we allow the authorized users to monitor and control from remote sites using hand held devices or web applications. Block chain can ensure the privacy and security of these applications. The communication between devices and control messages can be recorded in the distributed ledger.

The information can be verified at any point in time as there are no chances of corruption or deletion in the distributed ledgers. Any unauthorized transactions will be rejected automatically. Algorithms like AES would provide symmetric cryptography for confidentiality and hash functions can be used to verify the integrity of communication. All these would make the smart infrastructures robust.

Based on the cases we discussed above, we can conclude that the combination of IoT and Block chain is really beneficial only for a specific kind of applications. The outcome of this analysis has been given in the table which will help people about choosing block chain for their application (Table 6.1).

It is quite evident that to get the maximum benefits of any emerging trend we need to check out all the possibilities of combining them together. Various use cases have been analysed where the combination of block chain and IoT along with other disruptive technologies like Artificial Intelligence and Machine learning are providing the opportunities for next generation industrial application. Whenever a new technology emerges, every industrial sector attempts to utilize that which involves huge investment of money and efforts. When IoT applications are considered to be equipped with Block chain we need to do well research on the suitability of the specific use case. We may say that, the asset sharing networks, smart contracts and supply chain management are the most appropriate business areas where we can expect maximum benefits by the integration of IoT and Block chain.

Our preliminary work findings give reasons to be optimistic about enterprise IoT's growth. Respondents clearly believe in its power and companies are demonstrating their support through greater investment in IoT initiatives. With this shift,

Table 6.1 Suitability of block chain in different applications

Scenario	Go for block chain	Go for other options
Application is data intensive and it is used by huge number of users	If all the users have write access to the data base and there are problems of conflicts	If only a limited number of users have write access, you may use a centralized data base
Applications where multiple users involve in transactions	If a mutual trust is required among the users, block chain would make the validation of transactions simple	If mutual trust is not required distributed data base can be used instead of block chain
Applications using third party authorities	If the involvement of third party authorities is creating bottlenecks, block chain is recommended	If third party entities are making the process simple without overheads, they would be preferred
Applications with stable requirements	If the application requirements would not undergo major changes in the future	If there are very frequent updates in the core application, block chain may become an overhead
Availability of skill sets and other resources	When the company is fully equipped with required skill sets and potential to pursue with advanced technologies can go ahead with block chain	Companies who are unable to invest on multiple skill sets and running on strict budget may not find block chain feasible
Relationship with stake holders	If the internal and external stake holders are ready to adopt technical and organizational challenges of block chain integration, block chain can be considered	If the stake holders may not be able to quickly adopt to block chain or if they have threats for continuing in future, it is not advisable to go for block chains

enterprise IoT may soon deliver far more transformational change than the incremental improvements seen to date, particularly with respect to increased productivity, an improved customer experience, and the creation of innovative products.

6.6 Conclusion

This chapter addresses the design and implementation aspects of Enterprise IoT in a more business perspective rather than a technical perspective. While huge amount of efforts are required for planning and estimation of any kind of projects, it cannot be emphasized more for Enterprise IoT projects due to their multi-disciplinary requirements and challenges involved. It provides the reader an understanding about the series of actions to be done during the process of design and implementation. More importantly, the chapter elaborately discusses the implementation of IoT in modern times with the latest advancements in the technology such as Big data analytics, Artificial Intelligence and Block chain.

References

1. Conoscenti M, Martin JCD, Vetrò A (2016) Blockchain for the Internet of Things: a systematic literature review. In: Proceedings of the 3rd international symposium on Internet of Things: Systems, Management and Security (IoTSMS 2016), Agadir, Morocco, 29 November–2 December, pp 1–6
2. Dorri A, Kanhere SS; Jurdak R (2016) Blockchain in Internet of Things: challenges and solutions arXiv, arXiv:1608.05187
3. Siow E, Tiropanis T, Hall W (2018) Analytics for the Internet of Things: a survey, ACM Comput Surveys 1(1), Article 1. Publication date: January
4. https://www.seebo.com/iot-design/
5. https://dzone.com/articles
6. https://internetofthingsagenda.techtarget.com

Chapter 7
Enterprise IoT Development Platforms

Abstract This chapter illustrates the role of IoT platform in Enterprise application development. The IoT platform integrates various components of the solution from hardware to cloud application. An IoT platform plays an essential role in the development of complete Enterprise solutions. The manufacturing, industrial, agriculture, and supply chain sectors have started exploring vastly the benefits of remote monitoring of devices, tracking vehicles, predictive maintenance activities, collecting sensor data for real-time production analytics and to ensure that safety standards are followed. And in industries like retail, healthcare, hospitality, and travelling.

IoT Platform plays a vital role in building the end to end IoT application starting from data collection to improving customer experience. Personalized services to the customers, effective communication with them are significant revenue drivers and business success. This chapter analyses the need to use a well-built IoT platform and the potential consequences of using it appropriately. However, there are plenty of proprietary and open source solutions for Enterprise IoT platform. So, this chapter also addresses the very big question, "Which platform is suitable for my specific business problem or domain?"

Keywords Internet of Things platform · Middleware · AWS · Azure · Google cloud · Kaa · Oracle IoT · IBM Watson · ThingWorx

Learning Objectives

1. To understand the significance of an Enterprise IoT platform in the development process.
2. To learn the basic features and comparison of few commercially available IoT platforms.

L. S. Jayashree, G. Selvakumar, *Getting Started with Enterprise Internet of Things: Design Approaches and Software Architecture Models*,
https://doi.org/10.1007/978-3-030-30945-9_7

7.1 Introduction

An IoT platform is a combination of several services, tools, practices and features which enables development of an end to end Internet of Things solution in a more faster and efficient way it makes the process of connecting the physical world to cyber world a faster and smoother one. It has provisions to connect diverse hardware manufactured by different vendors to the cloud by a flexible connectivity method. It would provide the security mechanisms with the level expected by the enterprise applications and a vast data processing capability. In the development front it provides ready to use features which would quicken the application development. The platform ensures that scalability and is taken care of by following predefined patterns and standards. It is designed to handle large amounts of data from the device layer, customer interactions, and applications and process them to provide real time responses. It functions as a glue that connects all the components of the eco system. At present there are plenty of choices for IoT platform is available. Selecting the appropriate IoT platform primarily depends on the requirements of the Enterprise, the kind of hardware devices they use, their demands for real time decision making, custom reports, budget, business model and other similar parameters. This chapter tries to give a broad level glimpse of major platforms available and it discusses the merits and demerits of each of the platform.

7.2 The Middleware Layer

The term IoT platform can be defined only in an abstract manner and it may mean different according to the perspective of the person. When our concern is connecting remote devices to applications it is referred as middleware. According to Nakhuva, Bhumi and Champaneria, Tushar [1], the middleware is responsible for the interactions between the devices and the higher level application components which are not naturally compatible. So this is known as cloud enablement or IoT enablement.

Primarily the middleware takes control of data collection from the hardware which would follow different protocols and network technologies. It manages the remote device configuration, device management and other activities related to monitoring, controlling and updating the devices.

There are plenty of hardware manufacturers, third party applications and cloud service providers which are all to be integrated with the support of middleware. When an enterprise things about a business solution, it should not be highly dependent on the underlying hardware and complicated software. IoT middleware should take care of that (Fig. 7.1).

Modern IoT platforms have advanced features in hardware management as well as application management. They have versatile front ends for the users, advanced analytics dashboards, on device data processing capabilities and modern cloud

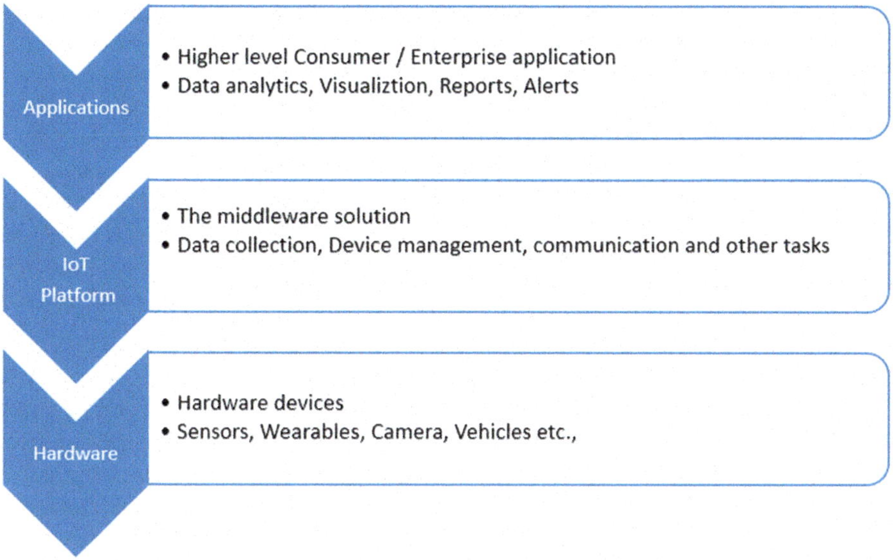

Fig. 7.1 IoT platform

based deployment. Most of them effectively provide end to end solution for Enterprises when they want to implement and IoT environment.

The primary requirement for middleware in Enterprise IoT is the standardization. Without standardization the IoT environment will be filled with silos where there is no opportunity for agility or scalability. At present, every vendor tries to build their product as innovative as possible and unique one. This should not stop building standards in the long run.

Another important requirement is robustness of the middleware. Both the front end device configurations and the backend systems are independently growing with their own technology advancements, the middleware should be able to handle all the changes dynamically. Any change should not hamper the role of Middleware for IoT that, its ability to act as a bond joining the mixed domains of applications communicating over a diverse range of devices and heterogeneous interfaces.

7.3 The Need for an IoT Platform

When people start with their IoT projects in companies, initially they think about creating the entire eco system by themselves. Instead of going to a platform which may cost a budget, people think about other alternatives such as building everything by their own. It may not be suitable for most of the Enterprises. The most common argument people have is that their product is a unique one and the ready made platforms may not address the requirements of their specific product because platforms address generic problems. This assumption is partly right, but the solution is looking for tools and services which would fill up the gap between their products and platforms. Not reinventing the entire wheel. And another point is that the platforms are developed by established companies and developers which ensures that the gaps would be filled in the subsequent releases [2]. The cost factor also plays an important role in neglecting the platforms. But when we consider in long term basis, it would cost very economical when compared to our own initiatives in building the entire system. We should not forget that the ready made platforms are built based on proven standards and best practices and they are made available after serious quality assurance routines. This section explains why IoT platform is required for Enterprises.

Complexity in the End to End Development Process
Designing and deploying end to end Enterprise applications are very complicated nowadays since starting from device management, connectivity service and application development has plenty of challenges when we approach them separately. Moreover, when they are handled individually, integration is always a time consuming and error prone process. Due to fragmentation of devices and the numerous choices of software technologies the inhouse teams usually unable to make quicker deployments. Skill gaps and lack of compatibility among the newer technologies increases the complications in developing and rolling the end to end IoT solutions. Existing cloud developers may need to undergo newer trainings which is also the case with many of the application developers. The learning curve is steep and addressing these problems will further delay the completion of the development.

The Significance of Data
Data is one of the most important drivers for IoT deployments. Cloud based IoT platforms provide several data management solutions readymade. Data storage, processing, analysing and other operations on the data can be done naturally on these platforms. Real time streaming data processing or batch processing, many of the platforms provide them by default. IoT platforms are preferred by the Enterprises because of this capability to integrating device management and data platforms effortlessly.

Security and Compliance
Customers embracing cloud-based IoT primarily because of security and compliance. From secure device provisioning and authentication to detecting vulnerabilities in connected devices, IoT PaaS is a secure platform. Public cloud vendors are offering guidance, and best practices for key players in the ecosystem including original device manufacturers, system integrators and software vendors building solutions and products. Mature cloud providers extend existing security and compliance of data platforms to IoT. TLS encryption, HIPAA compliance, SOC 2 Type 2 compliance and data sovereignty are some of the most sought out security features of IoT platforms.

AI and ML and Other Capabilities

Powerful technologies like Artificial Intelligence and Machine learning are becoming value additions for the IoT PaaS solutions. The Enterprises will be benefitted tremendously by these innovations in their objectives such as predictive maintenance. The advancements in the application layer can overcome the limitations in the device layer in the process of providing sophisticated services to the Enterprises. For example, a very basic surveillance camera can be used for more advanced image analysis without any requirement for frequent hardware update. In addition to that, IoT platforms provide AR and VR based solutions in several areas. Problem areas such as remote maintenance of machineries has involvement of augmented reality-based solutions along with IoT.

Edge Computing and Device Management Capabilities

Edge computing is changing the landscape of IoT development in the recent times and it is believed to be the next big thing in IoT. Latency and bandwidth usage are the primary challenges for cloud based IoT solutions. Many of the Enterprise solutions especially which are in the odd places cannot depends upon the cloud based IoT solutions due to the round-trip time taken to the cloud from device layer. When there are a greater number of sensors, the data generated would reach higher volumes which is another challenge.

Edge computing is addressing these issues by deploying an edge device that acts as a middleware between devices and the cloud. These are managed by the IoT control panel. These advancements can be materialized only with the help of well-defined platforms. The machine to machine communication, authentication, authorization and similar device level activities can be done by IoT PaaS. Device management itself has become very complicated due to the need for using bulk devices, scheduling and security requirements etc., These factors necessitates IoT platform.

Standardization

Being a new addition to the family of technologies, IoT experiences lack of standards. From simpler tasks to major processes there is a lack of standardization everywhere in IoT. There are several cloud service providers who never implement their solutions consistently. Since the area is evolving, these challenges are unavoidable. Communication among devices from different platforms is still a problem. Considering this, building end to end IoT solutions in-house would have serious problems on interoperability.

7.4 Selecting the Appropriate IoT Platform

There are several vendors providing IoT platform services in the market today. Some services are provided popular companies as proprietary solutions and several others as open source solutions. This section discusses the important factors to be considered before selecting the appropriate IoT platform [3]. The functionalities of all platforms are mostly similar. The differences are related to their other nonfunctional characteristics and their focus. Amazon's AWS IoT, Microsoft's Azure IoT, Google cloud platform are few of the top players in the industry. There are hundreds of open source platforms are also available.

The common capability of all these platforms is that they already take care of the infrastructure management. So the developers can focus only on the core application development. The enterprises should be getting the services from any of those providers and making that decision is quite complex. It involves the nature of various people in the enterprise such as Engineering, IT development, Finance etc., To make the process simple, here we provide few key factors to be considered.

The Vendor and the Ecosystem Provided by the Platform

The vendor should be a reputable organization and considerably a long term player to judge their services. Since IoT is just at its growing stage it poses enough risk too. Betting on a new player on the core business of an Enterprise is not a good option. The management of the enterprise should think about it and they should come up with a plan on how to evaluate the vendors. The track record, review from previous users, reputation, stability of their services everything should be evaluated properly. The IoT ecosystem has become so huge that one company may not be able to control everything. So the vendor should have a healthy partner ecosystem to enable providing more services of different nature and opportunity for collaboration.

The vendor should have clear understanding of the industry, so that the solution can be designed the specificity of the data, application requirements, business challenges and other similar things. Moreover, the company should have a team with strong expertise to train the people to use their platform by understanding the architecture and mastering the interfaces.

The Openness of the Platform, Interoperability and Extensibility

This is the age of flexible and convenient open APIs. Extensibility will be an important parameter in selecting the platform. The programmatic access to any given functionality is important for future scaling, interoperability with other systems and for easier understanding of the system. So, Enterprises should make sure that they select a provider that gives you programmatic access to as much of their functionality as possible.

The IoT platform should support as many protocols as possible for data integration. Zigbee, BLE, BACENET, MODBUS and there is a long list of protocols should be supported by the platform. The hardware devices are powered by various chipsets like MIPS based, ARM, x986 etc., The hardware agnostic approach of the platform is highly anticipated. It can be achieved by some of the latest technological breakthroughs like containerization. A particular set of functionalities are provided across a variety of different IoT hardware without no or very less changes.

Similarly, in the application tier side, the IoT platform should be capable of integrating with other peripheral systems of the organizations like ERP or supply chain management. This enables all the employees, business units and stakeholders of the Enterprise to have a synchronized view on the operations.

The Edge Intelligence

The future of IoT platform is progressing towards Edge computing. As we have already quoted in few places previously, intelligence of the system has to be distributed and offline to withstand the challenges in huge data transmission to cloud [4]. Only when the devices become more powerful, autonomous and quicker decisions can be made. So, The IoT platform should be able to support new topologies for decentralized computing. The ability to push updates to the edge applications over the air is very important. These kinds of updates should be possible to gateways, devices drivers and other components also. The platform should be capable of doing this.

Fault Tolerance and Security

Outage and fault can occur anytime in the IT infrastructure. A simple mistake can make the enterprise suffer because of unavailability of services. It may cost huge even though the fault lasts for few seconds or minutes. The faults can be either natural or man-made. The IoT platform should be able to handle those situations by taking sufficient and frequent backups of data. When something goes wrong, the platform should be ready with alternative procedures to terminate any faulty process smoothly and recover the operations as quick as possible.

Another important requirement for the platform is Security. DDoS attacks can break any system and hack the devices. The IoT platform should provide detailed methods for authentication, encryption and other measures to ensure the security. Role based access control, logging of user activities and errors are the other things to be taken care of by the platform.

Higher Level Services Provided by the Platform

Beyond basic services, there are plenty of value additions required to be provided by the platforms. These services are highly valuable according to the nature of business domains on which the platform is used. For instance, comprehensive analytics and advanced visualization is highly required for certain industries like finance management. General statistical analysis is common in almost all the platforms and visualization also has become a norm. However, certain industries need some advanced features. The platform should be able to support these functionalities by themselves or it should support adding the functionalities from third parties.

Edge computing capabilities is another advanced requirement from IoT platforms, because more and more enterprises have started adopting innovative edge computing. User management, security provisioning, ability to collaborate with auditing systems are some of the other features highly desired from the IoT platforms.

7.5 A Study on IoT Platforms

In this section, we just give a glimpse on few popular IoT platforms. The background of those platforms, primary services provided, merits and demerits are touched upon here. Choosing the right platform must be done only according to the nature of requirements in the Enterprise, rather than the profile of the platform. While the previous section addresses those parameters to be considered while choosing the platform, this section provides just a view on few platforms available at present.

Usually the platform to be chosen for an Enterprise development can be done by experts. They analyze the available IoT platforms by considering the Business and Pricing factors, Market Segmentation, Partner Ecosystems and the skill set requirements etc.,

7.5.1 Amazon's AWS IoT

Amazon has been providing IoT platform services to support Enterprises to make the development easier. Amazon's resourcefulness in the cloud makes it a prominent player in this sector. The AWS IoT platform is used to connect the IoT devices to the amazon cloud naturally. The AWS IoT platform is a combination everything we need to connect a microcontroller such as Arduino or Raspberry pi to the cloud with provisions to continuously collecting data from these devices and to supply them to the higher order applications. All the interactions are well secured by TLS. Support to C, JavaScript languages are available naturally which makes this platform an easier start for the enterprises [5].

Main Features of Amazon Web Services IoT

- The AWS IoT device gateway follows publish-subscribe model for messaging which makes multicast communication and one to one communication possible. Thousands of different devices can be connected through the gateway effortlessly. AWS IoT device SDK has to be installed with certificates and keys given by Amazon. MQTT messages communicate the data from device gateway to the other layers.
- X.509 standard is followed for device authorization and authentication procedures and it is done through AWS Signature version 4.
- A backup process known as device shadowing is followed in AWS in which the states of devices are preserved in the form of snapshots. The states can be restored again to the devices. The developer can inject the snapshots to devices and change their states. It is done through REST API. It can be even automated through rules engine. The rules engine is in the IoT backend service and the messages update the device shadows. Applications are usually communicating with the device shadows which are the representation of the actual devices. We can

control physical parameters like temperature for a thermostat from a mobile application or a dashboard in the laptop through proper authorization.
- AWS Lambda, Amazon kinesis are other popular AWS endpoints to which the data can be redirected. AWS rules engine takes care of application development by data collection, processing and other advanced operations. The Amazon end points can be connected to other open source visualization tools also.
- It does not even require that the physical device must be online during the change. Even though the device is offline, when it comes to online the change will take place. The rules engine transform messages to other services of Amazon.

Why Should Enterprises Consider Using AWS IoT?
- Amazon a major player in the industry provides state of the art security measures to protect the data in its cloud servers. Security is the foremost important requirement for an Enterprise application, and it is ensured by Amazon to the maximum.
- AWS provides multiple authorizations, authentications and cryptography techniques to make sure that the communication between IoT devices and the cloud is highly secure.
- The amazon's ecosystem is way better when compared to the other service providers. IAM – Amazon's authentication engine, AWS CloudTrail, a service that treats security problems and AWS Console are making the AWS IoT a great solution for Enterprise development.
- Amazon focuses more on start-up companies as they are going to be the future bigger companies, Amazon provides a very elaborate guide on how and where to start with using the SDKs and to reduce the costs. It also releases special startup packages like AWS Activate for start-ups. It publishes several success stories and interviews to encourage start up companies. The meet ups, blog posts, detailed documentation and other services provided by Amazon proves to be very effective and encouraging for the small enterprises to start with AWS IoT.

Thus, as per the reasons stated above, the AWS IoT platform is the first preference among several IoT Enterprises especially start-up companies. The vast and well matured infrastructure is the choice of developers who are working in IoT projects in Enterprises. It enables them to choose flexible options in terms of cost and other cloud-based services. Along with all these, security and stability have also been implemented in AWS with near perfection.

7.5.2 Microsoft Azure IoT

The Azure Internet of Things (IoT) is an IoT platform developed and managed by Microsoft. Billions of IoT devices and components are connected, monitored and controlled by the Microsoft cloud services. Along with that, there is a rich set of backend services also running in the Microsoft cloud for various advanced operations to support Enterprises. Some of the salient features of Microsoft Azure IoT are given below [6].

- Application developers have huge flexibility in the development and deployment processes. There are multiple deployment options where the developers can choose based on physical devices or cloud computing or hybrid.
- There is a very extensive built-in backup facilities available. The data is automatically backed up. The unstable network connection or major failure of computing devices or networks cannot make an Enterprise fail due to the robust backup capabilities.
- Emergency recovery capabilities provided by Azure IoT are very superior when compared to the other products. It also starte supporting implementation of applications with the latest technologies like blockchain.
- The efficiency of Azure IoT is highly remarkable due its state of the art data sorting and analytics features.

7.5.3 Google Cloud IoT

Google Cloud IoT is the service provided by the tech-giant Google. It has the complete set of tools to build an IoT ecosystem. The capabilities to connect, communicate, store, and analyse data is available at the edge as well as in the cloud. The platform consists of highly scalable cloud services. Also, it has integrated software stack for edge/on-premises computing with advanced features like machine learning. Here is the list of some important characteristics of Google Cloud IoT [7].

- The Google Cloud IoT has services like Google BigQuery for ad hoc analysis, Cloud Machine Learning Engine for advanced analytics using ML, Google Data Studio for very rich dashboard designs and report generation. Cloud IoT Core is responsible for data capturing. All these services combined together make Google Cloud IoT a well matured set of services for any Enterprise which tries to accelerate business agility and decision making.
- Google Cloud IoT supports a huge range of embedded operating systems. The devices from manufacturers like Intel, Microchip and other leading companies are supported. Automatic events are triggered using Cloud Functions workflow which can be connected to a variety of devices and operating systems to improve the operational efficiency.
- Google maps is a phenomenal service of Google which enables visualizing the location of assets in real time and their path of travel, frequency of movements etc., It may indoor or outdoor or any part of the globe, Google services integrated with Google maps help us to track them with precision.
- Google stands out from the rest with the help of its Cloud IoT core which has the ability to handle enormous amount of data.

7.5.4 Oracle IoT

Oracle IoT is another prominent IoT platform which can be integrated with Oracle PaaS. Connecting with almost all kinds of devices, real time analytics and the support provided by Oracle PaaS are the major benefits of using Oracle IoT. At present, it is being used in several retail, manufacturing, healthcare and industries. The following are some of the main feature of Oracle IoT [8].

- The ability for collecting and processing huge amounts of data is the main strength of Oracle IoT due to its large-scale data centers. Oracle Business Intelligence Data services has a very vast capabilities of management and analytics of collected data.
- Oracle Billing and Revenue management are the functionalities of Oracle which make it most suitable for integrating with extensive business applications like budget management. This feature is very much desirable in large enterprises.
- Oracle the owner of Java technology has the advantage of advanced java development support in its ecosystem.
- Oracle Database security is one of the most advanced security security mechanism in the industry which enables end to end overall safety for data.

7.5.5 IBM Watson

IBM has developed an IoT platform with rich set of features which is called as IBM Watson and it is one of the most powerful Internet of Things cloud platforms. The graphical user interface of Watson has been designed more effectively, so that, addition of new devise, changing the access level and controlling the behaviour of system more easily. The following are the most important features of IBM Watson [9].

- The real time is used for stream analytics based on various requirements and the previously transmitted information is stored in cloud storage for any further reference or operation in future.
- IBM Blumix is a powerful PaaS which can be integrated with Watson.
- IBM Watson has capabilities to handle slow networks and lower grade hardware.
- The developers can remotely reboot or update the firmware through IBM Watson remote control. All device configuration can be done with advanced remote-control mechanism more effectively when compared to other platforms,
- TLS protocol is used to make the data transmission more secure. It is easier to implement than IPsec. It is ideal for large number of gateways.

7.5.6 ThingWorx Industrial IoT

ThingWorx is an end to end technology platform especially designed for Industrial IoT. It is a complete suite of solution which has tools and technologies to empower Enterprises to quickly develop and deploy very effective applications [1]. The unique feature of this platform is its support to augmented reality (AR). The most important features of ThingWorx are given here [10].

- Vuforia based AR development is supported in ThingWorx. Kepware is available for industrial connectivity. KEPServerEX is another facility for data distribution. Thus ThingWorx is a suite of several services required for Enterprises.
- The programming activities required for ThingWorx is quite easier when compared to other platforms. The basic operations like establishing connection to the data source, configuration of device behaviors and interface design can be done without much programming tasks. This improves the turnaround time for simple use cases.
- Composer, Mashup Builder, storage and search tools, collaboration tools are available with ThingWorx which makes it a complete package for Enterprise IoT development.
- The Composer and Mashup Builder are used for modelling environment for design testing and the development of Mashup Builders. Thus common components like lists or buttons can be created easily.
- SQUEAL stands for Search, Query, and Analysis. SQUEAL is the search engine for ThingWorx. It analyses and filters data and functions as a searching tool for the records.

7.5.7 Kaa IoT Platform

Kaa is one of the very famous open source IoT platform which is considered to be the most flexible platform suitable for applications with any existing architecture. It is compatible with almost any type of connected equipment and supports real time data exchange. It is delivered under the free Apache 2.0 license. The following are some of the main features of Kaa IoT platform [11].

- As a open source platform kaa has no annual or service payments. Only the technical support and additional services are available as paid services. So it can benefit small Enterprises or start up companies with limited budget.
- The integration with third party solution is free and simple with Kaa.

- Kaa has completed around 20 years of existence in the market. So it is being supported by a larger developer community to support any possible problem in using Kaa for the Enterprises.
- Kaa gives few options for deployment of solutions. It may be on-premise, cloud hosted or hybrid.
- Kaa is a transport agnostic platform which may support any IoT protocol including lightweight IoT protocols such as CoAP.
- Applications can be built on top of persistent or intermittent connection.
- Kaa credential management API can be used for provision and suspension of valid credentials.

What has been presented above is just a short glimpse on the available platforms. The detailed list of their functionalities and their limitations can be seen from their corresponding websites.

7.6 Conclusion

The Enterprise IoT focuses on connecting very large number of devices, collecting huge amount of data and processing them which ultimately plays vital role in review generation of the Enterprise. So the IoT platforms developed for this purpose should be characterized by fault tolerance, stability, interoperability, security and extensive technical support. All these features are provided by the above platforms to a varying extent. The above-mentioned platforms are similar in their major functionalities and characteristics. All the platforms are providing services hosted on cloud that can yield great value from the data generated from the device layer and they offer advanced analytics and visualization services.

Apart from the major platforms discussed in this section, here is a list of other players who are also doing a remarkable job in the IoT platforms market.

- Datav by Bsquare
- Mindsphere by Siemens
- Ayla Network by Ayla
- ThingSpeak
- Bosch IoT Suite
- WebNMS IoT
- Exosite
- Carriots
- General Electric's Predix
- Xively
- MBED IoT Device platform
- Jasper IoT
- Arrayent
- Mosaic (LTI)
- Mocana

- Telit IoT
- ARTIK

The platforms are continually being modernized by the latest advancements in machine learning, artificial intelligence, NLP etc., So, in most of the scenarios they function quite similar. However, there are differences in areas like specialized set of services provided and the cost of utilization. All of them are continuously evolving with new features and the readers are suggested to read the corresponding websites to understand their latest offerings and limitation.

References

1. Nakhuva B, Champaneria T (2015) Study of various Internet of Things platforms. Int J Comput Sci Eng Survey 6:61–74. https://doi.org/10.5121/ijcses.2015.6605
2. PratimRay P (2016) A survey of IoT cloud platforms. Future Comput Inform J 1(1–2):35–46
3. https://www.mckinsey.com
4. https://www.saviantconsulting.com
5. https://aws.amazon.com/iot/
6. https://azure.microsoft.com
7. https://cloud.google.com/solutions/iot/
8. https://cloud.oracle.com/iot
9. https://www.ibm.com/watson
10. https://www.ptc.com/en/products/iot/thingworx-platform
11. https://www.kaaproject.org/

Printed by Printforce, United Kingdom